50 more
ACTIVE
ASSEMBLIES

Michaela Toske

PETER NORTON

Heinemann Educational Publishers
Halley Court, Jordan Hill, Oxford OX2 8EJ
a division of Reed Educational & Professional Publishing Ltd

MELBOURNE   AUCKLAND   FLORENCE   PRAGUE
MADRID   ATHENS   SINGAPORE   TOKYO
SÃO PAULO   CHICAGO   PORTSMOUTH (NH)
MEXICO   IBADAN   GABORONE
JOHANNESBURG   KAMPALA   NAIROBI

Heinemann is a registered trademark of Reed Educational &
Professional Publishing Ltd

01   00   99   98
10   9   8   7   6   5   4   3   2   1

British Library Cataloguing in Publication Data
A catalogue record for this book is available from the British Library

ISBN 0 435 30238 8

Cover designed by Threefold design
Designed by Artistix, Thame, Oxon
Typeset by TechType, Abingdon, Oxon
Printed and bound in Great Britain by The Bath Press, Bath

Acknowledgements
The publishers would like to thank the following for permission to
reproduce copyright material:

The Bible Society/HarperCollins Publishers Ltd for the Bible extracts
on pages 6–8, 18–20, taken from the *Good News Bible*, UK, ©
American Bible Society, 1966, 1971, 1976, 1992; The Children's
Society for the material on pages 27–29, adapted from The Children's
Society's *Christingle Celebration Service Guide*; Department of Trade
and Industry for the information on page 17, adapted from the
Fireworks Code; HarperCollins Publishers Ltd for the material on
pages 125–126, adapted from *Reach for the Sky* by Paul Brickhill;
Oxford University Press for the definitions of 'pride' on page 76,
adapted from the Oxford English Dictionary, 8th edition, 1991, by
permission of Oxford University Press; Roland Harvey Studios for the
material on pages 25–26, adapted from Roland Harvey's *New Book of
Christmas*; Wayland Publishers for the material on pages 14–15,
adapted from *Festivals Halloween* by Robin May.

The publishers have made every effort to trace copyright holders.
However, if any material has been incorrectly acknowledged, we
would be pleased to correct this at the earliest opportunity.

Contents

Introduction

In this second book I have continued to develop interesting and stimulating ideas for easy-to-use assemblies which generally involve pupils and make use of a wide range of visual aids.

The themes provided have been chosen for their varied content, ranging from those with a mainly religious meaning, to those which cover moral values. Many are common to all the world's major religions. Some of the assemblies cover themes that are related to other assemblies in the book. These are indicated at the end of the assembly under the heading 'Related assemblies'.

Each assembly has been provided with detailed notes so it can be delivered with the minimum of extra effort. You may wish, however, to take the ideas and adapt them to suit your own personal style.

Where the use of an overhead projector has been recommended, you may, if one is not available, make the provided resources (e.g. OHP 1 God sent the angel) into posters instead of transparencies.

A number of the assemblies contain plays. Given time to rehearse, these can be narrated and performed by pupils. As an alternative, if you wish you can narrate the play yourself and direct the pupils' actions as you go along. This reduces the time needed for rehearsals and allows you to retain more control of the pupils during the actual performance.

To enhance your assembly further you might wish to include a piece of music which is related to the assembly theme. Here are some ideas you may want to try:

Assembly	Music
January	'January' (Pilot)
Easter	*The Messiah* by Handel
Hallowe'en	'Ghost in the machine' (The Police)
Remember, Remember	Music for the Royal Fireworks by Handel
Christmas	'When a child is born' (Johnny Mathis)
Christmas around the world	'I believe in Father Christmas' (Greg Lake)
Christingle	'Gaudete' (Steeleye Span)
Chinese whispers	'I heard it through the grapevine' (Marvin Gaye)
Which hand?	'Band on the run' (Paul McCartney)
Environmental Blockbusters	'Born free' (Matt Munro)

Put your own house in order	'Big yellow taxi' (Joni Mitchell)
As dead as the Dodo	'Dodo' (Genesis)
The Christmas spirit	'Can't buy me love' (The Beatles)
Crime and punishment	'Crime of the century' (Supertramp)
Heads you win	'The gambler' (Kenny Rogers)
John's red Ferrari	'I have a dream' (Jason Donovan)
Noah's Ark	'Rhythm of the rain' (Cascades)
Into the lions' den	*Lion King* theme (Elton John)
Forty days of rain	'Winchester Cathedral' (New Vaudeville Band)
Patron saint of travellers	'It's nice to go travelling' (Frank Sinatra)
Doubting Thomas	'Thomas the rhymer' (Steeleye Span)
Everest	'Climb every mountain' (Julie Andrews)
Scott of the Antarctic	'Albatross' (Fleetwood Mac)
The lady with the lamp	1812 Overture by Tchaikovsky
Edith Cavell	*Casualty* theme (Ken Freeman)
The diary of Anne Frank	'Biko' (Peter Gabriel)
Robin Hood	'Everything I do' (Brian Adams)
Twm the Highwayman	William Tell Overture by Rossini
Douglas Bader	Battle of Britain March by William Walton

Where no piece of music obviously fits with the assembly theme title, there are a variety of pieces of contemporary or classical music you could choose because of the mood they create.

Celebrations

With this group of assemblies you have the opportunity to increase the pupils' awareness of a number of important celebrations.

Assembly	Theme
January	*New Year's resolutions*
Maundy money	*The traditions behind Maundy Thursday*
Easter	*The Easter story*
Hallowe'en	*Hallowe'en and its British traditions*
Remember, Remember	*Firework safety; the pointlessness of violence*
Christmas	*The Christmas story*
Christmas around the world	*Christmas traditions around the world*
Christingle	*The Christingle service and the message behind it*

January

Theme   New Year's resolutions

Date   The first week of the spring term

Materials
- OHP and screen
- OHP: New Year's resolutions

Before the assembly, write some examples of New Year's resolutions to project on the screen. For example:

Always work hard
Always do your homework
Think about your work during lessons
Take a pride in your work
Try to improve your writing

Be more helpful
Be kind to others
Take a pride in your appearance
Always tell the truth
Co-operate with others

Assembly organization   Start the assembly by asking the pupils if any of them have made New Year's resolutions. You might like to ask some of them to give examples of the resolutions they have made.

Go on to explain that making New Year's resolutions is one of many traditions related to the New Year, which is seen as a time for making a fresh start and resolving to improve.

Point out to the pupils that the month of January, being the start of a New Year, was first introduced by Julius Caesar as far back as 46 BC (over 2000 years ago).

The name for the first month, January, came from the Roman God Janus, who was the god of entrance and beginnings. This may be why the month at the beginning of the year was named after him.

Janus was a two-headed god, one head looking forward into the future and the other looking backwards into the past. This could have been related to the end of the year, when Janus looked back into the old year and forward into the new one. Today it is still traditional for television programmes to look back at the year just gone, as they welcome in the New Year.

Some other New Year's Eve traditions you might like to mention are:

The singing of Auld Lang Syne

The song 'Auld Lang Syne' was written by Robert Burns. Today it is a tradition, all around the world, to hold hands and sing this song as the New Year starts. The holding of hands probably dates back to an ancient Celtic New Year tradition of holding hands while dancing around a fire. The Celts believed that the flames would give them the strength to live through the cold dark winter months ahead.

First footing

Some people believe that the first person to come through their door (called the first footer) will affect the year ahead. According to tradition dark-haired men as first footers will bring good luck, especially if they are carrying a lump of coal (to signify warmth for the following months). It is thought to be unlucky if the first footer is flat-footed. (You might like to suggest that if you have blonde hair and flat feet you would definitely not be a welcome first footer!)

Hogmanay

In Scotland (where many British traditions come from) New Year's Eve is called Hogmanay, which may come from a French term about lucky mistletoe. In some areas of Scotland people would set fire to an old boat or a straw figure, which was believed to burn up the old year and make way for the New Year.

Next go on to tell the pupils that you want to return to the tradition that you started the assembly with, that is making New Year's resolutions, and that you want to set them some resolutions to keep during the year. Explain that the resolutions you want them to make are divided into two categories:

1 Academic (lesson) resolutions.
2 Personality (behaviour) resolutions.

and guide them towards giving the example you have prepared on the OHP.

As you bring out each of the resolutions uncover it on the OHP so it is projected for all the pupils to see. (If you wish you could dispense with the prepared material and simply write each resolution as the pupils mention them.)

When all the resolutions are displayed on the screen, give the assembly a minute to pick one resolution from each category (or to think of resolutions of their own which relate to each category).

Conclude the assembly by reminding the pupils that their resolutions should be improvements that they are going to make over the following months and that you hope that they will try to keep them.

Related assemblies None

Maundy money

Theme The traditions behind Maundy Thursday

Date In the last week of the Spring term (near Maundy Thursday)

Materials • Washing-up bowl and cloth

Before the assembly select a volunteer from your form to mime washing the feet of the pupils during the assembly. Set out at the front of the assembly as many chairs as your volunteer is years of age.

Assembly organization Start the assembly by choosing as many pupils as there are chairs at the front. Next ask your volunteer to act out his/her mime. When the volunteer has finished, ask the assembly if they can tell you what the mime was about. Bring out the answer: Washing people's feet.

Go on to explain that the mime they have just watched is related to Maundy Thursday. Ask the pupils if they can tell you exactly when Maundy Thursday is. Bring out the answer: The Thursday before Good Friday.

Next ask the assembly what traditional ceremony the Queen will be involved in on Maundy Thursday. Bring out the answer: She will be handing out Maundy money. Go on to explain a little more about Maundy Thursday traditions. Some points you might like to talk about are:

Medieval tradition The handing out of Maundy money originates from the medieval tradition in which the king or queen along with other nobles and priests would wash the feet of poor people and give them gifts of food, clothing and money. As in the pupil's mime, the king or queen would wash the feet of as many people as he/she was years of age.

Biblical connection Ask the pupils if they can tell you what event these traditions commemorate. Bring out the answer: When Jesus washed the feet of his disciples at the Last Supper, showing that no one is greater than anyone else (John 13: 1–20). You might like to mention that the name Maundy comes from the Greek word 'mandatum' which means mandate or commandment, as during the Last Supper Jesus gave his disciples the commandment to love one another (John 13: 34–35). Go on to point out that this is why Maundy Thursday is on the day before Good Friday, the night of the Last Supper.

Queen Elizabeth I Returning to the theme of Maundy Thursday itself, it is said that Queen Elizabeth I had the feet of the people washed before she washed them. (If you wish you might like to make some reference to 'smelly feet' at this point and suggest that you can understand her wish to have the people's feet washed first.) In 1572 she also gave things to the people: cloth to make some new clothes as well as bread, wine and fish.

Changing tradition The feet-washing tradition continued until the reign of James II (around 1680), who was the last king to wash people's feet. However, a slightly different version of the tradition did continue until 1754, in that the king or queen had someone else wash the poor people's feet on their behalf.

Today the Queen continues the modern Maundy Thursday tradition by giving a purse, containing specially minted silver coins for each year of her age, to one old man and one old woman.

Conclude the assembly by suggesting that the pupils might like to look out for some references to Maundy Thursday in the media (television, radio or newspapers), as they now have more idea about the significance of this day.

Related assemblies None

Easter

Theme The Easter story

Date In the week before the end of the Spring term.

Materials
- OHP and screen
- OHP 1 The arrest of Jesus (page 9)
- OHP 2 Jesus is sentenced to death (page 10)
- OHP 3 Jesus is crucified (page 11)
- OHP 4 The death of Jesus (page 12)
- OHP 5 The resurrection (page 13)

Before the assembly, when the above OHPs have been made into transparencies, colour in the main characters leaving everything else in outline only. This will give emphasis to these characters. You will also need to copy each of the five readings. Select five volunteers and give them time to practise their readings. For younger pupils you might like to have the readings retyped using large type.

Assembly organization Start the assembly by explaining to the pupils that you want them to listen to five readings from the Bible which tell the story of the crucifixion of Jesus.

Before each reading, project onto the screen the relevant OHP picture. After each reading you could elaborate on the story and tell the part of it that links the last reading to the next one.

Put OHP 1 on the screen.

Reading **The arrest of Jesus** Luke 22: 47–53

Jesus was still speaking when a crowd arrived, led by Judas, one of the twelve disciples. He came up to Jesus to kiss him. But Jesus said 'Judas, is it with a kiss that you betray the Son of Man?'

When the disciples who were with Jesus saw what was going to happen, they asked, 'Shall we use our swords, Lord?' And one of them struck the High Priest's slave and cut off his right ear.

But Jesus said, 'Enough of this!' He touched the man's ear and healed him.

Then Jesus said to the chief priests and the officers of the temple guard and the elders who had come there to get him, 'Did you have to come with swords and clubs, as though I were an outlaw? I was with you in the Temple every day, and you did not try to arrest me. But this is your hour to act, when the power of darkness rules.'

Put OHP 2 on the screen.

Reading **Jesus is sentenced to death** Luke 23: 13–25

Pilate called together the chief priests, the leaders, and the people, and said to them, 'You brought this man to me and said that he was misleading the people. Now, I have examined him here in your presence, and I have not found him guilty of any of the crimes you accuse him of. Nor did Herod find him guilty, for he sent him back to us. There is nothing this man has done to deserve death. So I will have him whipped and let him go.'

The whole crowd cried out, 'Kill him! Set Barabbas free for us!' (Barabbas had been put in prison for a riot that had taken place in the city, and for murder.)

Pilate wanted to set Jesus free, so he appealed to the crowd again. But they shouted back, 'Crucify him! Crucify him!'

Pilate said to them the third time, 'But what crime has he committed? I cannot find he has done anything to deserve death! I will have him whipped and set him free.'

But they kept on shouting at the top of their voices that Jesus should be crucified, and finally their shouting succeeded. So Pilate passed the sentence on Jesus that they were asking for. He set free the man they wanted, the one who had been put in prison for riot and murder, and he handed Jesus over for them to do as they wished.

Put OHP 3 on the screen

Reading **Jesus is crucified** Luke 23: 32–43

Two other men, both of them criminals, were also led out to be put to death with Jesus. When they came to the place called 'The Skull', they crucified Jesus there, and the two criminals, one on his right and the other on his left. Jesus said 'Forgive them, Father! They don't know what they are doing.'

They divided his clothes among themselves by throwing dice. The people stood there watching while the Jewish leaders jeered at him: 'He saved others; let him save himself if he is the Messiah whom God has chosen!'

The soldiers also mocked him: they came up to him and offered him cheap wine, and said, 'Save yourself if you are the king of the Jews!'

Above him were written these words: 'This is the King of the Jews.'

One of the criminals hanging alongside him hurled insults: 'Aren't you the Messiah? Save yourself and us!'

The other one, however, rebuked him, saying, 'Don't you fear God? You received the same sentence he did. Ours, however, is only right, because we are getting what we deserve for what we did; but he has done no wrong.' And he said to Jesus, 'Remember me, Jesus, when you come as King!' Jesus said to him, 'I promise you that today you will be in Paradise with me.'

Put OHP 4 on the screen.

Reading   **The death of Jesus** Luke 23: 44–49

It was about twelve o'clock when the sun stopped shining and darkness covered the whole country until three o'clock; and the curtain hanging in the Temple was torn in two. Jesus cried out in a loud voice, 'Father! In your hands I place my spirit!' He said this and died.

      The army officer saw what happened, and he praised God, saying, 'Certainly he was a good man!'

      When the people who had gathered there to watch the spectacle saw what happened, they all went back home, beating their breasts in sorrow. All those who knew Jesus personally, including the women who had followed him from Galilee, stood at a distance to watch.

Put OHP 5 on the screen.

Reading   **The resurrection** Luke 24: 1–7

Very early on Sunday morning the women went to the tomb, carrying the spices they had prepared. They found the stone rolled away from the entrance to the tomb, so they went in; but they did not find the body of the Lord Jesus. They stood there puzzled about this, when suddenly two men in bright shining clothes stood by them. Full of fear, the women bowed down to the ground, as the men said to them, 'Why are you looking among the dead for one who is alive? He is not here; he has been raised. Remember what he said to you while he was in Galilee: "The Son of Man must be handed over to sinners, be crucified, and three days later rise to life." '

Conclude the assembly by reminding pupils that at this time of year Christians around the world celebrate Easter and the resurrection of Jesus. Point out that this is the most important festival in the Christian calendar.

Related assemblies None

Hallowe'en

Theme   Hallowe'en and its British traditions

Date   In the week before Hallowe'en (31 October)

Materials
- Pumpkin lantern
- Bowl of water and apples

Assembly organization   Explain to the assembly that you want to look at the British traditions related to Hallowe'en. You will not be talking about 'Trick or Treat', which is an American tradition, apart from saying that if anyone does go out to play Trick or Treat, they should only go to the houses of friends and never to strangers' houses. They should also never go to the houses of elderly people, as they are often frightened by people playing Trick or Treat.

Next, talk about some of the festivals which Hallowe'en has replaced. Some information you might like to use would be:

- The name Hallowe'en still contains parts of the older festival name of All Hallows Eve, which was the night before 1 November on which day the church celebrated the feast of All Saints, when people remembered all the saints who had died. This was then followed on 2 November by the feast of All Souls, when all other people who had died would be remembered.
- In pagan times there had always been a festival of fire at this time which was called the festival of Samhain. This was the Celtic New Year.
- At this time of year, the Romans also held a festival in honour of the goddess Pomona, who was the goddess of fruits and gardens.

Go on to point out that many of the traditions we have today are based on a mixture of pagan and Christian origins.

Some traditions you might like to mention are as follows:

Mischief night   In Yorkshire and other northern counties Hallowe'en was also called 'Mischief night' because on Hallowe'en people would get up to all sorts of mischief. Hallowe'en was also the time when the Lord of Misrule was elected. It was his job to ensure merriment and enjoyment over the Christmas season, making the holiday during the hard winter months in the Middle Ages a happy time.

Apples   The use of apples in a variety of ways plays an important part of any Hallowe'en celebration. This tradition probably relates back to the Roman customs which were part of the festival of the goddess Pomona.

One popular game involving apples is called apple-bobbing (known as apple-dooking in Scotland). Apples are floated in a bowl of water and people try to pick them out using only their teeth. This led to the Lancashire name for Hallowe'en, 'Duck Apple Night', or on Tyneside, 'Dookie Apple Night'. (At this stage you might like to ask a few volunteers to come forward and try apple-bobbing themselves.)

It was also believed that on this night if a girl ate an apple while looking into a mirror at midnight, she would see an image of her future husband looking over her shoulder. Girls also used to stick apple pips on their cheeks. Each pip represented a boyfriend. The girl would then wait for the pips to fall off. The one that stayed on the longest showed her which boyfriend she would marry. (Once again, if you wanted to, you could bring out a volunteer to demonstrate this tradition.)

Hallowe'en fires

Hallowe'en was a festival of fires, when people lit fires for many reasons. For example, they believed the fires would help to ensure the sun's return next spring, and farmers hoped crops and animals would flourish. Today these fires have become part of the celebrations on 5 November (Bonfire Night) instead.

Hallowe'en lanterns

In Somerset (in the south of England), Hallowe'en is referred to as 'Punky Night'. The punkies are Hallowe'en lanterns made from mangelwurzels (a kind of beet). Show the pupils your pumpkin lantern and explain that in many parts of the country similar lanterns are made from pumpkins. Tell them how the lantern was made (if you wish you could also explain how the insides are then made into soups or pies). You could also point out that fires and lanterns were often made in the hope of keeping witches away.

Conclude the assembly by suggesting that this Hallowe'en the pupils, with their parents, might like to take part in some of the traditions you have mentioned, the easiest of which would be apple-bobbing or making Hallowe'en lanterns. Finally remind the assembly that following Hallowe'en, which has many of its traditions in pagan festivals, are two Christian festivals:

1 All Saints' Day (1 November) – when all the saints are remembered.
2 All Souls' Day (2 November) – when all faithful Christians of the past are remembered.

Related assemblies None

Remember, Remember

Themes Firework safety; the pointlessness of violence

Date In the week before 5 November

Materials None
N.B. The firework code information provided in this assembly should always be updated with any recent amendments.

Assembly organization Start the assembly by asking the pupils if anyone can complete this rhyme:

> Remember, remember
> The fifth of November.
> Gunpowder, treason and plot.

(I suggest you stop at this point and find a volunteer to complete the rhyme.)

> I see no reason
> Why gunpowder treason
> Should ever be forgot.

Then go on to talk about what it is they are remembering on Bonfire Night. This can be done by getting the pupils to answer the following questions.

1 Who is it we remember? *Guy Fawkes. (His proper name was Guido Fawkes.)*
2 What did he try to do? *Blow up the king and all the members of parliament.*
3 When did this happen? *5 November 1605.*
4 Why was he trying to do this? *Because Catholics (Guy Fawkes and the others were Catholics) were being discriminated against and were banned from worshipping in their own way.*
5 What happened to Guy Fawkes? *He was tortured and finally executed on 31 January 1606.*

Move on to explain that today's celebration came about because after the failed plot, Parliament ordered that 5 November should become a holiday. It was already customary to light Hallowe'en fires at this time and these soon became part of Bonfire Night. A few years after the plot, gunpowder explosions also became part of the celebrations and by the nineteenth century, roman candles and rockets were used.

Explain to the pupils that because of the tradition of fireworks on Bonfire Night, many people have been badly injured and some have even died, by not behaving in a sensible way. Because of these dangers the pupils would be best advised to go with their parents to an organized fireworks display.

However, if they are going to have some fireworks at home these are some rules for them and their parents to follow:

- Only their parents should light fireworks.
- Make sure the person lighting the fireworks follows the instructions.

(The instructions should be read by torchlight and not by lighting a match.)

- Light all fireworks at arm's-length using a slow-burning taper.
- Stand well back.
- Never return to a firework once it has been lit.
- Never throw fireworks (it is a criminal offence) or fool around with them in any way.
- Never put fireworks in your pocket.
- Keep all fireworks in a metal box with a lid.

At this point you might like to mention sparklers, which are usually given to children, and point out that at family parties these cause many injuries. Remind the pupils that sparklers, like fireworks, are dangerous, and if their parents do allow them to have sparklers they should :

- Wear gloves.
- Always hold them at arm's-length.
- Never put them near to anyone's face.
- Put the finished sparkler into a bucket of water.

Go on to remind the pupils that fireworks are very dangerous and that each year many people are injured by them. (In some years over 1000 people have been injured.) Therefore, whether they go to an organized display or have a few fireworks at home with their parents they should always be sensible and follow the Firework Code above.

Conclude the assembly by reminding the pupils that on 5 November we remember the failed attempt of Guy Fawkes to blow up the Houses of Parliament, an act which would have resulted in the death of lots of innocent people. We should remember that violence can never solve any disagreements. In the words of Britain's famous wartime leader, Winston Churchill: 'To jaw-jaw is always better than to war-war', which means it is better to talk about a problem than to fight over it.

Related assemblies None

Additional notes If you wish you could follow this assembly with a fireworks safety poster competition.

Christmas

Theme   The Christmas story

Date   In the week before the end of the Autumn term.

Materials
- OHP and screen
- OHP 1 God sent the angel (page 21)
- OHP 2 The birth of Jesus (page 22)
- OHP 3 The angel visits the shepherds (page 23)
- OHP 4 The visit of the kings (page 24)

Before the assembly, when the above OHPs have been made into transparencies, colour in the main characters leaving everything else in outline only. This will give emphasis to these characters. You will also need to copy each of the four readings. Select four volunteers and give them time to practise their readings. For younger pupils you might like to have the readings retyped using large type.

Assembly organization   Start the assembly by explaining to the pupils that you want them to listen to four readings from the Bible which tell the story of the birth of Jesus. Before each reading, project onto the screen the relevant OHP picture. After each reading you could elaborate on the story and tell the part of it that links the last reading to the next one.

Put OHP 1 on the screen.

Reading   **God sent the angel** Luke 1: 26–33

In the sixth month of Elizabeth's pregnancy God sent the angel Gabriel to a town in Galilee named Nazareth. He had a message for a young woman promised in marriage to a man named Joseph, who was a descendant of King David. Her name was Mary. The angel came to her and said, 'Peace be with you! The Lord is with you and has greatly blessed you!'

     Mary was deeply troubled by the angel's message and she wondered what his words meant. The angel said to her, 'Don't be afraid, Mary; God has been gracious to you. You will become pregnant and give birth to a son, and you will name him Jesus. He will be great and will be called the Son of the Most High God. The Lord God will make him a king, as his ancestor David was, and he will be the king of the descendants of Jacob for ever; his kingdom will never end!'

Put OHP 2 on the screen.

Reading   **The birth of Jesus** Luke 2: 1–7

At that time the Emperor Augustus ordered a census to be taken throughout the Roman Empire. When this first census took place, Quirinius was the governor of Syria. Everyone, then, went to register himself, each to his own town.

Joseph went from the town of Nazareth in Galilee to the town of Bethlehem in Judaea, the birthplace of King David. Joseph went there because he was a descendant of David. He went to register with Mary, who was promised in marriage to him. She was pregnant, and while they were in Bethlehem, the time came for her to have her baby. She gave birth to her first son, wrapped him in strips of cloth and laid him in a manger – there was no room for them to stay in the inn.

Put OHP 3 on the screen.

Reading   **The angel visits the shepherds** Luke 2: 8–20

There were some shepherds in that part of the country who were spending the night in the fields, taking care of their flocks. An angel of the Lord appeared to them, and the glory of the Lord shone over them. They were terribly afraid, but the angel said to them, 'Don't be afraid! I am here with good news for you, which will bring great joy to all the people. This very day in David's town your Saviour was born – Christ the Lord! And this is what will prove it to you: you will find a baby wrapped in strips of cloth and lying in a manger.'
    Suddenly a great army of heaven's angels appeared with the angel, singing praises to God:
    'Glory to God in the highest heaven,
    and peace on earth to those with
    whom he is pleased!'

When the angels went away from them back into heaven, the shepherds said to one another, 'Let's go to Bethlehem and see this thing that has happened, which the Lord has told us.'

So they hurried off and found Mary and Joseph and saw the baby lying in the manger. When the shepherds saw him, they told them what the angel had said about the child. All who heard it were amazed at what the shepherds said. Mary remembered all these things and thought deeply about them. The shepherds went back, singing praises to God for all they had heard and seen; it had been just as the angel had told them.

Put OHP 4 on the screen.

Reading   **The visit of the kings** Matthew 2: 1–12

Jesus was born in the town of Bethlehem in Judaea, during the time when Herod was king. Soon afterwards, some men who studied the stars came from the east to Jerusalem and asked, 'Where is the baby born to be the king of the Jews? We saw his star when it came up in the east, and we have come to worship him.'

When King Herod heard about this, he was very upset, and so was everyone else in Jerusalem. He called together all the chief priests and the teachers of the Law and asked them, 'Where will the Messiah be born?'

'In the town of Bethlehem in Judaea,' they answered. 'For this is what the prophet wrote:
>   "Bethlehem in the land of Judah,
>   you are by no means the least of
>   the leading cities of Judah;
>   for from you will come a leader
>   who will guide my people Israel."'

So Herod called the visitors from the east to a secret meeting and found out from them the exact time the star had appeared. Then he sent them to Bethlehem with these instructions: 'Go and make a careful search for the child, and when you find him, let me know, so that I too may go and worship him.'

And so they left, and on their way they saw the same star they had seen in the east. When they saw it, how happy they were, what joy was theirs! It went ahead of them until it stopped over the place where the child was. They went into the house, and when they saw the child with his mother Mary, they knelt down and worshipped him. They brought out their gifts of gold, frankincense, and myrrh, and presented them to him.

Then they returned to their country by another road, since God had warned them in a dream not to go back to Herod.

Conclude the assembly by reminding the pupils that at this time of the year Christians around the world celebrate the birth of Jesus, upon whose life and death the Christian religion is built.

Related assemblies None

Christmas around the world

Theme   Christmas traditions around the world

Date   Any time during December

Materials
- OHP and screen
- Two maps (the world and Europe) made up into transparencies. Copies of both of these will be readily available within the school.

Before the assembly you might like to arrange for a group of pupils to practise singing the first verse of the carol 'Good King Wenceslas'.

Assembly organization   Start the assembly by pointing out to the pupils that the Christmas festival that many people in Britain will be celebrating soon is one that is celebrated by many millions of people in different countries all over the world. Go on to explain that in today's assembly you want to look at some of the things people in other countries do as part of their Christmas celebrations.

Put the OHP map of Europe on the screen.

For each of the countries listed below ask if anyone can come up and show the assembly where that country is on the map. If you feel the pupils would not be able to do this, then indicate yourself where each country is located.

France   In France, shortly before Christmas, the family sets up a special nativity scene. In some households the children put their shoes by the fireplace to be filled with presents by Père Noel (Father Christmas). It is also traditional in some parts of the country to put a large log on the fire and keep it burning from Christmas Eve until New Year's Day.

Italy   The Italian Christmas season lasts for three weeks, beginning eight days before Christmas. Many Italian people fast (go without food) for twenty-four hours before Christmas Day. At midnight they attend Mass, then end their fast with a special supper of panetoni (spiced bread) and chocolate.

Denmark   For Danish people Christmas Eve is the most important day. On Christmas Eve the family puts presents under the tree, and nobody is then allowed into the room until after the evening meal of roast goose. They also have a tradition of hiding an almond inside a Christmas pudding, and the person who gets it receives a large marzipan pig. (Many years ago people in England used to hide a silver coin inside Christmas puddings.)

One Danish legend has it that on Chrismas Eve a mischievous elf called Nisse has his fun. Families leave bowls of rice pudding or porridge out on Christmas Eve to try and please Nisse so that his jokes are not too extreme.

Czech and Slovak Republics (These countries used to be the one country of Czechoslovakia.) Christmas is a quiet religious day for the Czech and Slovak people. At night on Christmas Eve most people go to Holy Mass (Pasterka) in churches which are full of Christmas trees and evergreens. For Christmas-Day dinner many people eat baked carp.

The traditional Christmas carol 'Good King Wenceslas' is based on a true Czechoslovakian king who was murdered by his jealous brother. Before dying, he asked God to have mercy on his brother. (If you have a group to sing the first verse, they could sing it now.)

Russia Start by asking the pupils what is the main difference between the Russian Christmas and ours. Bring out the answer: Russians celebrate Christmas Day on 7 January.

On Christmas Eve many Russian families eat a twelve-course supper in honour of the twelve Apostles.

Baboushka is the Russian traditional person who gives presents to children at Christmas time.

Change the OHP map to the map of the world.

Australia Christmas in Australia comes in the middle of their summer. Many people who originally came from Europe still eat the traditional roast turkey lunch and then go off to the beach for a swim.

Conclude your assembly by reminding the pupils that however the millions of people around the world celebrate Christmas, the one thing they are all celebrating is the birth of Jesus.

Related assemblies None

Additional notes Good King Wenceslas looked out, On the Feast of Stephen, When the snow lay round about, Deep and crisp, and even: Brightly shone the moon that night, Though the frost was cruel, When a poor man came in sight, Gath'ring winter fuel.

Christingle

Theme   The Christingle service and the message behind it

Date   Early December

Materials
- OHP and screen
- OHP 1 Christingle orange (page 29)

The following items are needed to make a Christingle orange (multiply the quantities so that each form present in the assembly can have a Christingle orange for their classroom):

- A candle.
- An orange with a hole (the circumference of the candle) cut in the top.
- A red ribbon with some cellotape to attach the ribbon to the orange.
- Four cocktail sticks with different small fruits (monkey nuts and raisins).
- A chair for each form present in the assembly.

Before the assembly ask each form to nominate one pupil to help during the assembly.*

Assembly organization   At the start of the assembly put the chairs at the front and and arrange on each of them the items for a Christingle orange. Begin by asking the volunteers from each form to come out to the front and stand by a chair. Explain to the volunteers and the assembly that you want to start by playing a simple game. Each volunteer at the front will have to decorate their orange with the ribbon and place the candle into it, then put the sweets and nuts onto the four cocktail sticks and stick them into the orange, to make the best decorated orange.

Put OHP 1 on the screen.

Allow the volunteers a few minutes to look at OHP 1 (giving them an idea of what the finished orange should look like) and make their decorated orange. Once they have all finished, get them to sit on their chair and hold the orange in front of them. (If you wish you could then award prizes for the best orange, or you could give each volunteer a small prize for taking part.)

Explain to the assembly that the oranges that have been made are part of a traditional Christian service, called the Christingle

* Ensure none of the pupils has a nut allergy.

service, which goes back over 200 years. The first Christingle service was believed to have been held in about 1747 in a country called Moravia; it was held by Pastor John de Watteville. In the twentieth century the idea of the Christingle service was re-introduced by John Pensom of the Children's Society.

You might like to go on to explain the Christian significance of the different elements of the Christingle orange, which are as follows:

- The word 'Christingle' means Christ-light.
- The orange is a symbol of the love of God in creating the world.
- The four cocktail sticks are symbols of the love of God in the four seasons.
- The fruits and sweets are symbols of the love of God in providing the food grown on Earth.
- The red ribbon is a symbol of the love of God in Jesus's death and resurrection.
- The lighted candle is a symbol of the love of God by sending his only son Jesus (the Light of the world).

I suggest that for safety reasons you explain that in church the candles would be lit and carols sung by their light, but that they should not light the candles themselves.

Conclude the assembly by sending the volunteers back to give the Christingle orange to their form teacher, so it can be kept in their classroom to remind them of the Christingle service and its meaning.

Related assemblies None

Our effect on others and the world around us

These assemblies provide the chance for you to encourage the pupils to think about those that are less fortunate than we are, and the effect we are having on the environment.

Assembly	**Theme**
Chinese whispers	*The harmful effects of gossip*
Do unto others	*Kindness towards others*
Which hand?	*Looking for the good in others*
The Vandals	*The unacceptability of vandalism*
Environmental Blockbusters	*The importance of environmental protection*
Put your own house in order	*Environmental damage to the British countryside*
As dead as the Dodo	*Respect for all living things*

Chinese whispers

Theme   The harmful effects of gossip

Date   No specific date

Materials
- Two phrases to use as Chinese whispers:
  Russian rabbits running round
  My auntie has a black hat with a feather
- Five chairs set a few feet apart at the front of the assembly

Assembly organization   Start the assembly by gathering at the front five volunteers from the assembly and asking them to sit on the chairs at the front. (You would be wise to avoid picking any pupils who might introduce any unacceptable words into the phrases. You may also want to include in your volunteers a pupil you have primed to introduce a change into your sayings.)

Explain to the assembly that today you are going to play a game called Chinese whispers. Go over to the first volunteer at one end of the line of chairs and whisper one of your two phrases. Let each volunteer in turn get up and go over to the next pupil and whisper the phrase. Continue this process until the last pupil has passed on the phrase. At this point ask the last volunteer to tell the assembly the phrase he/she has been told.

Next, gather another five volunteers and either repeat the process using your second phrase or use both phrases and start them from opposite ends of the line. After playing both games of Chinese whispers, contrast the phrases repeated to the assembly with the original phrases you started with.

Now go on to relate the game of Chinese whispers to the habit some people have of gossiping, and point out that although Chinese whispers is fun, gossip is often very unpleasant and upsetting for the person who is being talked about. You might like to contrast gossip with a conversation about a friend's recent success, which is an acceptable topic of conversation provided it is not exaggerated or talked about in any unpleasant way.

Go on to explain two ways in which gossip can become upsetting for the person who is being talked about:

1 People who gossip about someone rarely have anything nice to say. They are usually talking about something unpleasant that has happened to the person or something he/she would not like everyone to know.
2 Gossip usually contains a number of things that are not true, either because someone is only passing on part of what they

have heard and are filling in the bits that are missing, or because they simply want to 'liven' up the conversation and so are adding in little bits to the story to make it more interesting.

You could relate back to your original game of Chinese whispers, again pointing out the difference between the original phrase and the one heard by the last pupil in the line.

Go on to point out that when people gossip about someone the person who is being talked about often gets to hear what is being said, either because:

- They overhear someone's conversation.

or

- Someone claiming to be a friend (and trying to be nice) tells them what is being said about them. (You might like to add that as a friend it would be better not to tell the person what is being said, but try to stop the rumours being spread.)

Conclude by pointing out that gossip is a very unpleasant use of language and that no one likes people gossiping about them. Remind the pupils of the saying 'Do unto others as you would have them do unto you', and that just as we wouldn't like other people gossiping about us so we should not gossip about other people.

If you wish you could also mention the ninth commandment, which states

'You should not accuse anyone falsely' (Exodus 20: 1–17) which, you could explain, means you should not say things that are untrue about anyone.

Finally, point out that a good rule to follow would be:
'Only say things about a person that you would be happy to say to that person's face.'

Related assemblies None

Do unto others

Theme   Kindness towards others

Date   No specific date

Materials   ● Four large sheets of paper, each with one of the following sayings written on it in large letters:

    1 Do unto others as you would have them do unto you.
    2 You reap what you sow.
    3 People who live in glass houses should not throw stones.
    4 Put yourself in the other person's shoes.

Assembly organization   Start the assembly by gathering at the front four volunteers to hold up your sayings. Ask the assembly what they think the first three sayings mean. For each saying, some points you might like to bring out are:

Do unto others as you would have them do unto you.
You should behave towards other people as you would like them to behave towards you. If you are nice to them, they will be nice to you. This is an idea that can be found in the Bible (Matthew 7: 12); if you wish you could read this to the pupils.

You reap what you sow.
You get back what you put into a situation. If you are nice to other people, they will be nice to you.

People who live in glass houses should not throw stones.
Point out that this saying is not actually about people throwing stones. Its real meaning is that if you do something unpleasant to someone they might do the same to you and that would upset you. So if you are not unpleasant towards anyone else then they will not be unpleasant to you.

Ask the assembly what these three sayings have in common. Bring out the answer: If you are nice to other people they will be nice to you.

Next return to the idea of not being unpleasant to other people. To do this look at the fourth saying and talk about the meaning behind it.

Put yourself in their shoes.
Explain that this does not really mean putting someone else's

shoes on. Its real meaning is to imagine how someone else must be feeling. How would you feel if the same thing was happening to you? If you are nasty to someone it will upset them and they will be unhappy, just as you would be upset if someone was nasty to you. Therefore, if you would not like something being done to you, then do not do it to someone else. This was the point of the first three sayings.

Conclude by bringing out the two main points of the assembly:

1 No one likes it if people are nasty to them (e.g. calling them names); everyone finds this upsetting.
2 Do not do to other people things that you would not be happy for them to do to you.

Instead of being nasty and calling each other names, we could all try to be nice to each other and then the world would be a much nicer place.

Related assemblies None

Which hand?

Theme   Looking for the good in others

Date   No specific date

Materials   • Two tennis balls

Assembly organization   Start the assembly by asking the pupils if they can tell you what the following list of famous people have in common. (If you wish, after reading out each name ask someone to tell you why that person is famous.)

Julius Caesar	*Roman emperor*
Jimmy White	*Snooker player*
Dawn French	*Comedienne*
Leonardo da Vinci	*Painter*
Martina Navratilova	*Tennis player*
Paul McCartney	*Musician*

Bring out the answer: They all are (or were) left-handed.

Then tell the pupils that you want to ask them some questions to think about, but not to answer:

• How many of them are left-handed?

(Point out that in fact about ten per cent of the population are left-handed.)

• How many of those who are left-handed have been teased or called names because of it?
• How many of those who are not left-handed have teased or called left-handed people names?

Explain to the assembly that whether you are left- or right-handed depends on which side of your brain is dominant. If you are right-handed, the left side of your brain is the dominant side. If you are left-handed, the right side of your brain is the dominant side.

Go on to point out that there are about forty activities which can be used to test which side of your brain is dominant and that very few people remain left- or right-handed throughout all of them. (Further information on this subject can be found in the book *Manwatching* by Desmond Morris.) Explain to the assembly that you would like them to try some of these tests:

• Scratch the centre of your back. Which hand does the scratching?

- Interlock your fingers. Which thumb is on the top?
- Fold your arms. Which arm is uppermost?

(For a little bit of fun you could ask the pupils to try and fold their arms the other way round.)

- Look at the person next to you. Wink at them. Which eye did the winking?
- Count up to three on your fingers. Which forefinger does the counting?
- Point at a distant object in the room. While pointing at the object, close one eye. While still pointing at the object, open that eye and close the other eye. Through which eye, when it is opened, is your finger pointing at the object?
- Put your arms behind your back, and take hold of one arm with the other hand. Which hand does the clasping?
- Ask two pupils, one who writes with his/her right hand and the other who writes with his/her left hand, to stand up. Pass a tennis ball to each pupil. Ask them one at a time to throw the ball back to you. Which hand do they throw it back with?

Throughout these tests the answer to the questions will indicate whether the pupils are left- or right-handed in each of the activities. Conclude this part of the assembly by asking the pupils how many of them remained right- or left-handed in every test.

Go on to point out that we all show elements of left-handedness and so it is as silly to tease someone about being left-handed as it would be to tease them about being left-eye or left-arm dominant.

In the same way, it is silly to tease someone about wearing glasses. In fact this is something that, as the saying goes, may come back to haunt you, as later in life you may have to wear glasses yourself and you would not be happy being teased by other people.

Conclude the assembly by pointing out that instead of picking on people's slight differences and using them to tease and bully, we should be looking at each other's strengths and successes and building on these.

Related assemblies None

The Vandals

Theme The unacceptability of vandalism

Date No specific date

Materials None

Before the assembly you will need to arrange for a number of volunteers from your form to practise acting out the three scenes of vandalism mentioned in this assembly.

Assembly organization Start the assembly by explaining to the pupils that you want to talk to them briefly about a group of people who lived over 1000 years ago.

Some points you mention are:

- They were a tribe of people who originally came from around the area today called Denmark and that they lived during the time of the Roman Empire.
- They invaded Gaul (now known as France) and even conquered land as far down as northern Africa.
- As they conquered towns and villages they would often, for no reason, destroy things, setting fire to buildings, even churches, and burning books.

At the end of your brief talk ask the pupils which word comes from the behaviour of this group of people. Bring out the answer: The Vandals or vandalism. Go on to explain to the assembly that vandals or vandalism are words we use today to describe people who behave like the ancient Vandals, wilfully or maliciously destroying things for no obvious reason.

Ask your first group of pupils to act out the vandalism of a telephone and telephone box. Then ask the assembly what they think these pupils were doing. Bring out the answer: Vandalizing a telephone and telephone box. Go on to point out some of the consequences of this action. Some points to bring out might be:

- These actions could put people's lives in danger if they needed to use the phone in an emergency.
- The damage must also be repaired and the cost of these repairs is added to everyone's phone bills through increased telephone charges.
- The materials used in the repair wastes resources.

Ask your second group of pupils to act out the vandalism of a tree sapling. Then ask the assembly what they think these pupils were doing. Bring out the answer: Vandalizing a tree sapling. Go on to point out some of the consequences of this action. Some points to bring out might be:

- There is a financial cost for everyone as the trees, if they are on public land, have to be replanted by the local council. This work is funded by local taxpayers.
- If the trees were not replaced this would have an adverse effect on the environment, as trees not only provide a habitat for lots of animals, they also help to clean up our atmosphere.

Ask your third group of volunteers to act out setting fire to the rubbish in a litter bin. Afterwards ask the assembly what they think these pupils were doing. Bring out the answer: Setting fire to rubbish in a litter bin. Go on to bring out some of the consequences of their act of vandalism. Some points to bring out might be:

- Once again their action might cost everyone money as the bin would be damaged and need replacing, which would require money from everyone's local taxes.
- Burning rubbish pollutes the atmosphere.

After talking about these examples of vandalism, ask the pupils to give you some examples they have seen locally. With each one talk about how the vandals' actions cost money for the whole society and how their actions have an adverse effect on the environment.

Having talked about some examples of vandalism given by the pupils you could, if you wish, talk to the assembly about any recent acts of vandalism that have occurred in the school and point out how these affect all the pupils and the environment.

Finally, remind the pupils how mindless acts of vandalism by a few people affects everyone:

- The repair costs for vandalism to public property have to be paid indirectly by everyone. (At this point you could introduce the idea of vandalism being anti-social behaviour as it affects all members of society.)
- Vandalism adversely affects the environment by wasting resources and increasing pollution.

Conclude the assembly by reminding the pupils that they should never take part in any acts of vandalism, not only because it affects everyone else in society but also because it affects our environment, which is being damaged enough by people's thoughtless actions.

Related assemblies None

Environmental Blockbusters

Theme   The importance of environmental protection

Date   No specific date

Materials
- OHP and screen
- OHP 1 Blockbusters board (page 41)
- Red and blue OHP pens

Assembly organization   Start the assembly by explaining to the pupils that today you are looking at a number of environmental matters and that you want to do this by playing a game of Blockbusters. Go on to outline to the pupils how you are going to organize your game:

1 The assembly is divided into two halves.
2 Each half is given a colour (red or blue).
3 A volunteer from each side will pick a letter from the hexagon grid (starting from the left).
4 If they answer the question correctly you will colour in the hexagon with their group's colour.
5 If the answer is wrong you will pass the question over to the other side.
6 If the other side answer it correctly the hexagon will be coloured in their group's colour.
7 If that side cannot give the correct answer, the question will be left blank until it is picked again.
8 To win, a complete connected set of hexagons of the same colour must be produced from left to right.

The rules
- Each half of the assembly will be asked one question each time.
- Only one person can give an answer for each question.

Put OHP 1 on the screen.

Flip a coin to decide which half of the assembly should start. Begin the game, colouring in the hexagons with the appropriate colour until one side wins.

Game questions   **D**   Which D are being killed when people fish with nets for tuna? *Dolphins*

E   Which E means no more members of the species left alive? *Extinct*

N   Which N is the form of waste that remains dangerous for thousands of years? *Nuclear*

O   Which O is the layer of gas being destroyed by aerosol gases? *Ozone*

W   Which W are the group of marine mammals which have been hunted for their meat? *Whales*

R   Which R is being killed by poachers for its horn? *Rhinoceros*

CD   Which CD is believed to be causing the greenhouse effect, in which the Earth's climate may be changing? *Carbon dioxide*

AP   Which AP describes the unpleasant effect of substances being put into the Earth's atmosphere? *Air pollution*

TRF Which TRF is the habitat being destroyed for the supply of timber? *Tropical rain forest*

S   Which S is sometimes pumped untreated into rivers and seas killing fish? *Sewage*

AR   Which AR is caused by gases dissolving in rainwater? *Acid rain*

T   Which T is being forced towards extinction because of its use in oriental medicines? *Tiger*

G   Which G is a large ape in danger of becoming extinct? *Gorilla*

FF   Which FF are being burned every day polluting the Earth's atmosphere? *Fossil fuels*

H   Which H being lost is leading to many plants and animals becoming extinct? *Habitat*

C   Which C causes air pollution in cities? *Car*

P   Which P is used by gardeners and is endangering the existence of some plant species? *Peat*

Once the game has been won, read out any unanswered questions and bring out the correct answers by asking a number of volunteers. You might, if time allows, like to explain some of the correct answers with additional information of your own.

Conclude the assembly by pointing out to the pupils that matters covered in this assembly represent some of the adverse effects human beings are having on Planet Earth. As its guardians we should not destroy it but instead do everything we can to protect it and hand it on to future generations with all its beautiful creations intact.

Related assemblies   As dead as the Dodo
Put your own house in order

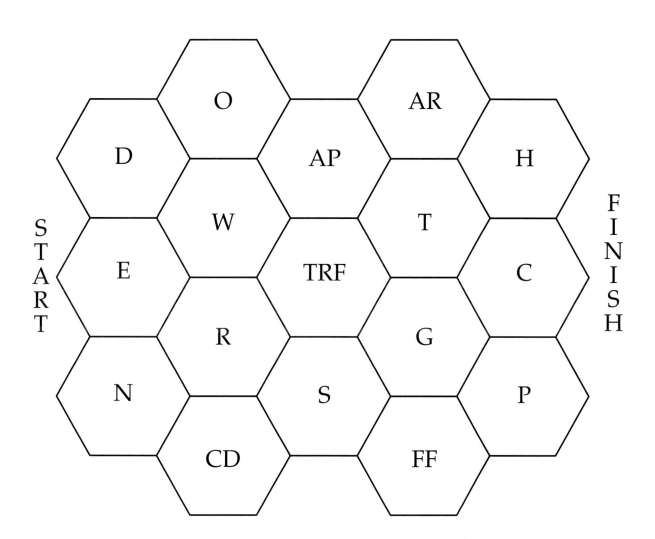

Put your own house in order

Theme   Environmental damage to the British countryside

Date   No specific date

Materials
- Six large sheets of paper, each with one of the following words written on it in large letters:

Put your own house in order.

Assembly organization

Start the assembly by gathering six volunteers at the front. Give each volunteer one of the sheets of paper and ask him/her to hold it up so that the assembly can see the word. (Make sure that the words are given out in the wrong order so as not to reveal the saying.) Ask for another volunteer to come forward and to rearrange the words to make a saying. (If you wish you could use a member of staff.)

Once the words have been rearranged into the saying, ask the pupils what they think it might mean. Bring out the answer: If you are criticizing someone for doing something, you should first ensure that you do not do the same thing yourself.

Next go on to ask the pupils to give you some examples of the world's present environmental concerns. Some examples to bring out might be:

- Destruction of the rain forests.
- Global warming.
- Acid rain.
- Pollution of the seas and oceans.
- Species extinction, e.g. tigers, elephants, etc.

Go on to point out to the pupils that these are all examples of worldwide environmental concerns, which they and other people in Britain would say we should do something about.

Relate these concerns back to your original saying by pointing out that while we are correct to express our concerns about these problems, we should ensure that we have 'put our own house in order' first and we are doing as much as we can to improve our own environment.

Follow this by pointing out a number of ways that you feel we are not doing as much as we can to improve the global environment and the British countryside itself. Some examples might be:

Global warming/ Acid rain

Are we doing enough to cut back on Britain's contributions to global warming and acid rain? Could we cut back further on our use of electricity and cars? (With younger pupils you might like to explain how these things are connected to global warming and acid rain.)

Destruction of the British countryside

Many features of our countryside are disappearing:

- *Peat bogs*. These are special wetland environments which were formed thousands of years ago. As the peat is dug up for use by gardeners, the plants and animals that live in this environment are in danger of becoming extinct. Since 1945 up to 96 per cent of Britain's peat bogs have been destroyed.
- *Hedges*. Over the last century, farmers have removed thousands of miles of hedges to make bigger fields. This has removed the habitat that many different species depend upon. As a result, birds such as the bullfinch are becoming increasingly rare.
- *Wildflower meadows*. These have been destroyed because of the changes in methods of farming, and because of this many species of butterflies and other insects, which feed on the flowers, as well as the flowers themselves, are becoming increasingly rare. Since 1945 up to 97 per cent of Britain's wildflower meadows have disappeared.
- *Deciduous forest*. Over the centuries thousands of native deciduous and evergreen trees have been cut down and whole woodlands have disappeared; this destruction is still going on today. This may be one of the reasons why species such as the red squirrel are becoming increasingly rare.
- *Heathland*. These are special areas which contain few trees but lots of heather. They are disappearing as a result of new roads and house-building as well as overgrowth of trees. This means the habitat is lost and the species which depend upon it (for example, birds like the Hobby and Dartford warbler) are becoming increasingly rare.

Conclude the assembly by pointing out that people in Britain are correct to express their concerns regarding worldwide environmental problems, but we should also ensure that, in the words of the saying, we 'put our own house in order' first. We should try to do what we can to be certain that as well as expressing concern about worldwide environmental issues, we also do everything possible to improve Britain's environment. If you wish you could end the assembly by introducing the saying 'think global, act local', which was introduced by environmental groups to get people not only to be aware of worldwide environmental problems but also to take action to improve their local environment.

Related assemblies

Environmental Blockbusters
As dead as the Dodo

Additional notes

If you wish you could follow this assembly with projects to improve the school environment, e.g. planting wildflowers and trees.

As dead as the Dodo

Theme   Respect for all living things

Date   No specific date

Materials
- OHP and screen
- OHP 1 As dead as the .... (page 46)
- Eight large sheets of paper, each with one of the following names written on it in large letters:

Passenger pigeon	Dodo	Woolly mammoth
Tyrannosaurus rex	Cheetah	Humpback whale
Giant panda	Orang utan	

Assembly organization   Start the assembly by gathering eight volunteers at the front and giving each one an animal name to hold up. From the eight animal names displayed at the front, bring together the following four:

Passenger pigeon	Dodo
Tyrannosaurus rex	Woolly mammoth

Ask the assembly what these names have in common. Bring out the answer: They are all extinct. (If they don't know the meaning of 'extinct' you can explain that it means that all the animals of one type are dead and have gone from the Earth forever.) You may like to give a little extra information about each of the four animals.

Passenger pigeon   This bird lived in North America and was once one of the world's most abundant birds. It died out because of over-hunting and the loss of its habitat. It is thought that the last passenger pigeon died in 1914.

Dodo   This large flightless bird once lived on the island of Mauritius in the Indian Ocean. It was finally hunted to extinction in about 1680. The early explorers had hunted it for food on their long journeys.

Tyrannosaurus rex   This large flesh-eating dinosaur (it measured approximately 7.5 metres in height) lived about 70 million years ago. According to one theory it became extinct when a large meteorite hit the Earth.

Woolly mammoth   This large hairy elephant lived in the colder parts of the Northern Hemisphere. It became extinct about 10,000 years ago as the Earth's climate warmed.

Ask the pupils what the passenger pigeon and the dodo have in common. Bring out the answer: They both became extinct because of the actions of humans. (You might like to add that the mammoth and the Tyrannosaurus rex both died out because of climate changes which humans had nothing to do with.)

Next bring forward the remaining four names:

Cheetah   Humpback whale   Giant panda   Orang utan

Ask the assembly what these four animals have in common. Bring out the answer: They are all in danger of becoming extinct. Once again you might like to give a little additional information about each animal.

Cheetah   They live in areas of Africa and are the fastest land animal, reaching speeds of over 100 kilometres per hour. They are in danger of becoming extinct due to loss of their habitat.

Humpback whale   This large member of the whale family is unusual in that it 'sings songs', using different notes each year. No one knows exactly why they sing. They have been hunted almost to extinction for their meat, which some people eat, as well as for their blubber to make cosmetics.

Giant panda   They live in an area of southern China, feeding on a diet of mainly bamboo. They are in danger of becoming extinct (there are possibly only 1000 pandas alive today) due primarily to the loss of their habitat.

Orang utan   They live in the rain forests of Borneo and Sumatra. The name Orang utan means 'man of the forest' in Malay (the language of the region). They are in danger of becoming extinct due to the loss of their habitat.

At this point you could ask the assembly to tell you the names of any other plants or animals that are in danger of becoming extinct.

Put OHP 1 on the screen.

Ask if anyone can complete the saying. Bring out the answer: As dead as the Dodo. Go on to point out that it would be a dreadful shame if these four animals and the thousands of other plant and animal species in danger were to become extinct like the Dodo due to the actions of humans around the world.

Conclude the assembly by pointing out to the pupils that although many of these plants and animals come from countries thousands of miles away, it is important that the whole world's population respects the lives of all living things and does everything it can to protect them and prevent them from becoming extinct.

Related assemblies   Environmental Blockbusters
Put your own house in order

AS DEAD AS THE _____ .

Personal qualities

This group of assemblies enables you to talk to the pupils about the development of a number of desirable personal qualities.

Assembly	Theme
Honesty is the best policy	*The importance of honesty*
Manners maketh humans	*The value of good manners*
The magic word	*Politeness and good manners*
The boy who cried wolf	*Not telling lies*
As plain as the nose on your face	*Tell lies and you will be caught out*
The Christmas spirit	*Making the best of life*
The grass is always greener	*Being thankful for what you have got*
Patience is a virtue	*The value of being patient*
Poacher turned gamekeeper	*Changing character for the better*
Crime and punishment	*What is wrong is wrong*
The devil finds work	*Making good use of your time*
Heads you win	*The danger of gambling*
Pride comes before a fall	*Taking pride in what you do*
Fools rush in	*The importance of thinking before you act*

Honesty is the best policy

Theme   The importance of honesty

Date   No specific date

Materials   None

Assembly organization   Start the assembly by asking the pupils if anyone can complete this saying: 'Honesty is the ...'. Next go on to ask the assembly for some examples of dishonest behaviour that they should avoid.

Talk briefly about each example to bring out the importance of being honest and to establish the idea that it is wrong to be dishonest. (To do this you might like to concentrate on the effect their actions have.)

Then go on to ask the pupils what happens if you get caught being dishonest. Bring out the facts: If it is something trival, e.g. eating some sweets at home that were not yours, then you may get told off by your parents and they may ban you from watching television for a couple of days; If it is more serious, like stealing from a local shop, you will be in trouble with the police and could end up in court (or even in prison). So honesty is the best policy, because if you get into trouble with the police it could affect the rest of your life and you could end up spending a great deal of your life in prison.

Now ask the pupils if they can think of another way that you can be dishonest in school. (Give them the clue – being dishonest with yourself.) Bring out the answer: By cheating in lessons or in tests. Ask if they have heard the saying, 'Cheats never prosper'. Explain that you want to spend the rest of the assembly looking at the truth behind this saying.

Start by asking the pupils what they think the word 'prosper' means in this saying. Bring out the answer: Do well. Now reintroduce the saying as 'Cheats never do well'.

Next ask the pupils to give you some examples of the ways people might cheat in school. (After each example talk about how this action demonstrates the saying 'Cheats never do well'.) Some examples might be:

- copying someone's homework

In this case, you will not have learnt how to find the information out yourself. You will also probably not be able to do the same work when you are tested in an exam. In addition it may also be obvious you have been cheating when the teacher marks your work, so you will get caught out and be in trouble.

- writing the answers on your hand before a test

You may not have written out the things you are actually asked in the test, so when you see the test questions you may still not be able to answer them. You may also get caught cheating in the test, and then your test will not be marked so you will have failed that piece of work. More importantly, if you cheat in school tests you will not have learnt how to revise and get ready for exams. Therefore, in final school exams when it is not possible to cheat you will not do as well as you might have done.

After talking about a few examples, go back to the saying and remind the pupils that, for the reasons you have given, 'Cheats never do well'.

Conclude the assembly by reminding the pupils that at all times and in all ways, 'Honesty is the best policy', and that they should never cheat, but always try their best at whatever they have to do. No one would ever expect any more than that each person should do their best.

Related assemblies None

Manners maketh humans

Theme The value of good manners

Date No specific date

Materials None

Assembly organization Start the assembly by asking the pupils what they should do in certain situations, for example:

- If they see someone approaching a door carrying something in both hands. *Open the door*
- What should they say to someone who helps them. *Thank you*
- What should they say if a group of people is in their way and they need to get past. *Excuse me*

Ask the pupils how they would describe the correct way to behave in each of these situations. Bring out the answer: Be polite and well-mannered.

Go on to explain to the assembly that there are many occasions when it is important to be polite and well-mannered. For example, how would they like to sit next to this person at the dinner table. (Mime, or arrange for a pupil from your form to mime, someone eating with appalling manners.)
  Draw the pupils' attention to some of the examples of bad manners demonstrated in the mime, e.g. eating with your mouth open, leaning across the table, using your fingers to eat, etc.

Next ask the pupils what they should do to be polite if someone is talking to them. Bring out the answer: Look at the person and pay attention to what they are saying. Go on to mime, or arrange for a pupil from your form to mime, someone who is not listening properly (looking away, yawning, talking to someone else) and contrast this with someone who is listening intently (looking at the person talking, showing interest, not interrupting). Explain to the assembly that listening with interest to someone who is talking to you not only means you are being polite and well-mannered but also makes it more likely that you will understand what you are being told and be able to remember it. (If you wish, you could suggest that the pupils remember to be well-mannered next time a teacher is talking to their class.)
  Finally go on to talk about other examples of impolite behaviour they should avoid (after each example explain the correct, polite way to behave):

- Not covering their mouth when yawning.
- Interrupting someone when they are talking to someone else.
- Burping in public.

Conclude the assembly by reminding the pupils that they should always behave in a polite and well-mannered way. If you wish you could introduce the saying, 'Manners maketh man'. However, you may wish to point out that this saying is not just talking about men but is referring to all humans (men and women), at which point you could reintroduce the saying as 'Manners maketh humans'. Then go on to explain that this saying is intended to remind us that being well-mannered and polite is one of the things that separates us from the animal kingdom, and so we should always strive to be well-mannered.

Related assembly   The magic word

The magic word

Theme Politeness and good manners

Date No specific date

Materials
- Packet of biscuits

Assembly organization
Start the assembly by explaining that today you want to look at the ways you can get people to help you and do things for you. Tell two pupils to come out to the front of the assembly. (Do it in an authoritarian manner.) Point out that when you are in a position of authority it is possible to order people to do things.

Ask the pupils to give you some examples of people who give orders that they expect people to follow. Some examples to bring out might be:

- Teachers
- Police officers
- Soldiers

Tell the two pupils who came out to the front to go and sit down. Point out that ordering people about is not a good way to get them to help you.

Next pick up the packet of biscuits and start to open them. While you are doing this, ask for two volunteers to come out to the front. When the two chosen pupils get to the front, ask them why they volunteered. Bring out the answer: They thought/hoped they might get a biscuit. Send them back and explain that you did not actually say they would get a biscuit. They were, of course, tricked into coming out and this also is not a good way to get people to help you.

Go on to explain that you will give your next volunteers a biscuit. Pick two volunteers and get them to come out to the front and give them a biscuit. Ask the assembly what method you used to get these two volunteers to come out to the front. Bring out the answer: Bribery. Explain that this is also not a good way of getting people to help you.

Explain that now you want to look at two totally unacceptable ways of getting people to do things for you:

1 Using threats – saying, for example, 'if you don't bring me a packet of sweets tomorrow, I'll hit you.'

Ask the assembly what this type of behaviour is called. Bring out the answer: Bullying. Then go on to point out that under no circumstances is bullying an acceptable way to behave.

2 Pressurizing someone to do something – for example, calling them a 'chicken' if they don't do something you want them to. This is called 'peer (friends) pressure' and is usually used to make you do something you know is wrong, like stealing.

Explain that peer pressure is very difficult to resist, but if people are trying to get you to do something that is wrong, you must resist it. (You might also like to suggest that if their so-called friends are putting pressure on them to do something wrong, then they are not very good friends.)

Point out to the assembly that so far you have not come up with any acceptable ways of getting people to do things for you. Ask the pupils: if they want someone's help, what is the best way to get it? Bring out the answer: By politely asking them.

At this point you could introduce the idea of using the magic word. Ask the pupils: what is the magic word? (You might like to point out that you don't mean abracadabra!) Bring out the answer: Please. Go on to explain that 'please' is called the magic word because if you use it people will normally help you. So it is the best way of getting people to help you.

Conclude the assembly by reminding the pupils that if they want people to help them, the best way to do it is to ask politely, remembering to say 'please' and not forgetting to say 'thank you' afterwards. (At the end of the assembly, you might like to give a biscuit to all the pupils who helped you.)

Related assembly   Manners maketh humans

The boy who cried wolf

Theme Not telling lies

Date No specific date

Materials None

Before the assembly you will need to recruit five volunteers from your form to play the following parts in the mini-play.

young boy   woman chopping wood
man and woman walking   man sawing wood

You should also find time for them to practise their actions.

Assembly organization At the start of the assembly organize your volunteers at the front so that they are ready to play their parts in the mini-play. Explain to the assembly that you want them to watch a short play, which has been adapted from a children's story.

Narrator Here we see a mischievous boy walking through the woods

○ *Boy stands up and starts walking around in front of the assembly. Woman stands up and starts to mime chopping wood.*

Narrator The boy saw the woman chopping wood. He crept up behind her and shouted ...

○ *Boy creeps up behind the woman and shouts 'There's a wolf!' Woman runs away screaming in terror.*

Narrator Later on his walk, the boy was following a couple walking through the woods.

○ *Couple stands up and starts walking around. Boy walks up behind the couple and starts to follow them.*

Narrator The boy crept up behind the couple and shouted ...

○ *Boy creeps up behind the couple and shouts 'There's a wolf!' Couple runs away screaming in terror.*

Narrator As the boy continued on his walk he saw a man sawing wood.

○ *Man stands up and starts to mime sawing wood. Boy walks over behind the man.*

Narrator The boy crept up behind the man and shouted ...

○ *Boy creeps up behind the man and shouts 'There's a wolf!' Man runs away screaming in terror.*

Narrator   A few days later the boy was again walking through the woods

○   *Boy continues walking around in front of the assembly. Woman, couple and man return to their initial positions at the start of the assembly and continue with their mimes.*

Narrator   As he walked through the woods this time, the boy realized he was being followed by a real wolf and he shouted ...

○   *Boy looks behind him and with a look of fear shouts 'There's a wolf!' Woman, couple and man continue with their actions. Boy collapses onto the floor and puts up his arms to protect himself.*

At this point ask the assembly what happened to the boy. Bring out the answer: He was eaten by the wolf. Go on to explain to the assembly that this is not a true story. It comes from the story of 'The boy who cried wolf', one of *Aesop's Fables*. As with many old stories of this type it was first told to give a moral message.

Ask the pupils what they think the message in this story might be. Bring out the answer: Do not tell lies or people will not believe you, even when you are telling the truth. Go on to relate this to everyday incidents involving the pupils. For example, those who are always in arguments and claim that the others started it or those who always have excuses for not doing their homework. When these pupils do have a genuine problem with other people picking on them or a genuine reason for not being able to do their homework, then people are less likely to believe them even though they are telling the truth.

Conclude the assembly by reminding the pupils that unlike the little boy in the story, they should not keep 'crying wolf' because when they do have a real problem and tell people the truth, they will not be believed because of the lies they have told in the past. If you wish you could also point out that not only should they not tell lies because people would not believe them when they do tell the truth, but they should also not tell lies because it is wrong. You could relate this to the ninth commandment: Do not accuse anyone falsely (Exodus 20: 1–17).

Related assembly   As plain as the nose on your face

As plain as the nose on your face

Theme   Tell lies and you will be caught out

Date   No specific date

Materials
- Old school-uniform tie (or any other tie if the school does not have a uniform)
- Sharp pair of scissors

Before the assembly you will need to practise the teacher/pupil sketch (below) with a volunteer from your form.

Assembly organization   Start the assembly by asking your volunteer to come to the front of the assembly. Give him/her the tie to put on. Next explain to the assembly that you want them to watch the following imaginary situation of a teacher asking a pupil why he/she has not handed in their homework and to see how the pupil deals with this problem. The action takes place over the space of a few days. Turn to your volunteer and start the following dialogue. (After each lie told by the pupil cut off a piece of the tie.)

Teacher Where is your homework?
Pupil   I have left it at home, Mr Smith.
Teacher Make sure you bring it in next lesson.
Teacher (*Turning to the assembly*) Next lesson ... (*Turning to the pupil*) Where is your homework?
Pupil   It was in my pocket ready to bring in when my Mum put my trousers in the wash, Mr Smith.
Teacher Here is another piece of paper. Make sure you have the homework done for next lesson.
Teacher (*Turning to the assembly*) Next lesson ... (*Turning to the pupil*) Where is your homework?
Pupil   It was on the table ready for me to bring in this morning when my little brother spilt juice all over it, Mr Smith.

If you wish you can continue this sequence for a little longer with additional lies which should become more and more unbelievable, or you can stop at this point and ask the assembly what the boy is doing. Bring out the answer: Telling lies. Ask the pupils if they think the teacher believed the boy's lies. Bring out the answer: No.

Allow your volunteer to go and sit down. Then point out that as the pupil continued to tell lies they became more and more unbelievable. In fact, the lies became 'as plain as the nose on his/her face', in the same way that the tie stood out more and more each time a piece was cut from it. Ask the pupils if any of them have heard that saying used in relation to lies and go on to explain its meaning as being the more you tell lies the more and more obvious they become.

Next ask the assembly if any of them can tell you the name of a character from a Disney cartoon whose lies were 'as plain as the nose on his face'. Bring out the answer: Pinocchio. Go on to explain that when Pinocchio and Jiminy Cricket were found with Stromboli by the Blue Fairy, Pinocchio started to tell lies as to how they got there and as he did so his nose got bigger and bigger.

Conclude the assembly by pointing out to the pupils that when they tell lies their nose will not grow bigger and bigger as Pinocchio's did, but the lies they tell will become more and more obvious as they try harder and harder to get themselves out of trouble, and so it is best that they do not start telling lies in the first place.

If you wish you could end by pointing out that even if you can get away with telling lies, it is still not a sensible thing to do as no one is going to want a friend who is well known for telling lies.

Related assembly   The boy who cried wolf

The Christmas spirit

Theme   Making the best of life

Date   In the weeks before Christmas

Materials   None

Assembly organization   Start the assembly by explaining to the pupils that today you want to look at a message about life that can be found in the famous Christmas book *A Christmas Carol*. Ask the assembly who wrote this book. Bring out the answer: Charles Dickens

Move on to the next part of the assembly by exploring the children's knowledge of the book using the following series of questions.

1 Who is the story about?   *Ebenezer Scrooge*
2 What sort of person was Scrooge? *Greedy and mean*
3 What was the name of his clerk?   *Bob Cratchit*

Go on to explain that the story starts on Christmas Eve with Bob Cratchit working in a cold, dimly lit room. Scrooge, who describes Christmas as being 'Humbug' (nonsense), complains to Bob about having to give him a day off work on Christmas Day. Later that evening Scrooge is visited by his late business partner Jacob Marley, who returns as a ghost to tell Scrooge to mend his ways.

Ask the pupils what came after Marley. Bring out the answer: Three ghosts. Ask the assembly which ghost came first. Bring out the answer: The ghost of Christmas Past. Go on to explain that this ghost took Scrooge on a journey to remind him of the simple enjoyment Scrooge had at Christmas when he was young.

Ask the pupils which ghost came next. Bring out the answer: The ghost of Christmas Present. Go on to explain that this ghost took him to the Cratchit's household, where he saw the simple enjoyment they shared at Christmas and how happy Bob's young son Tiny Tim was, despite his poor state of health and crippled legs. Scrooge asks the ghost what will happen to Tiny Tim. The ghost tells him that unless the Cratchit's life improves he will die.

Ask the assembly which ghost comes next. Bring out the answer: The ghost of Christmas Yet To Come. Go on to explain that this ghost takes Scrooge to see his own neglected grave and the Cratchit family mourning the death of Tiny Tim.

When Scrooge awakes he opens his window and asks a small boy what day it is. It is Christmas Day. The ghosts had visited him during the night and there was still time for him to make the best of this Christmas and to change his ways.

In conclusion there are three points you can bring out (you can choose to cover all of them or concentrate on one):

- At Christmas especially, but throughout the year as well, it is important to think of others and not just to think of yourself. Scrooge, after the visit by the three ghosts, took more notice of the difficulties of Bob Cratchit's family (with his weak and crippled son Tiny Tim). So he increased Bob's wages and tried to help his family. You could relate this to the saying 'It is better to give than to receive'. If you wish you could explain that this idea comes from the Bible (Acts 20, 35).
- To enjoy Christmas (or any time) you do not have to have expensive gifts or lots of money; there can be just as much enjoyment from the simple things in life. This was shown by the Cratchit family who made the best of what they had at Christmas and still enjoyed themselves. You could relate this to the saying 'It's the thought that counts' (rather than the size of a gift).
- Having money is not a guarantee of being happy. Rich people are not always as happy as those with far less money. Despite all his money, Scrooge was not happy because he did not know how to enjoy himself. You could relate this to the words of the Beatles song 'Can't buy me love'.

Conclude the assembly by reminding the pupils that at Christmas and all the year round, they should be like Tiny Tim and enjoy every bit of life despite any problems they may have. Most of all they should not be like Scrooge and miss out on enjoying life by being miserable and not entering into the spirit of things.

Related assembly   The grass is always greener

The grass is always greener

Theme   Being thankful for what you have got

Date   No specific date

Materials

- Seventeen large sheets of paper, each with one word from the following two sayings written in large letters:

  The grass is always greener on the other side of the fence
  Keeping up with the Jones's

Assembly organization

Start the assembly by picking 17 volunteers to come to the front of the assembly and hold up the words to make up two famous sayings. Give each volunteer one of the words from your two sayings and arrange them in a line in front of the assembly. (Make sure the words are not displayed in the correct sequence.) Ask the pupils to hold up their words for the rest of the assembly to see.

Ask the rest of the assembly if any of them can rearrange the words to make two famous sayings. Anyone who feels they know the sayings can come forward and attempt to arrange the words in the correct order. (Staff could also be asked to come forward and try.) Once the pupils/words have been arranged into the correct order ask the volunteers to read out the two sayings.

Ask the assembly what theme the sayings have in common. Bring out the answer: They are both to do with being greedy or envious. Go on to talk about each of the sayings in turn and explain a little more about their meanings. Some points to mention are outlined below.

The grass is always greener on the other side of the fence.
Ask the pupils what might be important about the grass being greener. Bring out the answer: Greener grass is better grass. Go on to explain that the saying is suggesting that things always look as though they are better for someone else. What they have seems better than what you have. Their life seems better than yours. But the main point behind the saying is that in fact things are not always better for someone else, and that no matter what you have in life it is always possible to see someone else who has something else that you wish you had.

Keeping up with the Jones's.
Ask the assembly what this saying means by the Jones's. Does it really mean Mr and Mrs Jones? Bring out the answer: It means neighbours or friends. Go on to explain that the saying refers to some people's efforts to keep up with the things their friends and

neighbours have or the things they do and it is intended to bring out the unhappiness that comes from trying to keep up with other people, instead of being yourself and doing what you want (or can afford).

Ask the assembly if anyone can give you a theme common to both of the sayings. Bring out the answer: Not to be envious of other people's possessions or lives and to be content with your own life. If you wish you could relate this last point to the tenth commandment, which says:

Do not envy another person's possessions (Exodus 20: 1–17).

Finish this part of the assembly by asking the pupils to suggest a saying that is better for people to follow than these two, one which encourages them to always look at the good things in their lives. Bring out an answer something like: Look on the bright side of life.

Conclude the assembly by reminding the pupils that rather than looking at what other people have it would be better to look at the good things they have themselves. To be envious of other people can only lead to unhappiness. (You might also like to point out that although the things people have may look better, it does not mean those people are any happier than anyone else.)

Related assembly   The Christmas spirit

Patience is a virtue

Theme   The value of being patient

Date   No specific date

Materials   None

Assembly organization   Stand or sit at the front of the assembly where you can see all the pupils. Do not say or do anything, just remain still at the front of the assembly, ensuring that the pupils sit still and quietly. Remain like this for as long as you can keep the pupils quiet and orderly. After a short time (about five minutes) ask the pupils which personal quality they have been showing. Bring out the answer: Patience.

Ask the pupils if they can think of a saying related to patience. Bring out the answer: Patience is a virtue. Explain that this means that patience is a good thing to have.

Next ask the pupils to tell you of some situations where patience is needed. Some examples might be:

- Waiting for a bus.
- Waiting at the doctor's/dentist's surgery.
- Queuing in a supermarket.

You might like to explain the possible consequences of losing your patience in the situations they have mentioned. For example:

- Waiting for a bus – after a while you give up waiting and start to walk. Just after you have left the bus stop the bus comes along and you miss it. As a result you have to walk all the way home.
- Waiting at the doctor's/dentist's surgery – when some people have to wait for too long in the surgery they may start to argue with the receptionist. This could result in them being removed from the doctor's or dentist's list and them having to find another surgery to go to.
- Queuing in a supermarket – when some people see how long the queues are they leave their trolley and walk out. They have wasted all that time shopping and they will still have to go somewhere else to get their food.

Go on to point out that sometimes when people lose their patience they become angry, and then an argument may start, which can even lead to a fight and someone getting hurt. In traffic jams, people often become impatient and then try to make up the time they have lost by driving fast, which can result in an accident and one or more people getting seriously hurt.

Conclude the assembly by pointing out to the pupils that although they will need to show patience in life, they will not need to show 'the patience of Job', which is a saying that comes from the Bible (James 5: 7–11). Job was a character in the Old Testament who showed the greatest patience possible in enduring the suffering in his life (Job: 1–42). Finally point out that, as you have explained in the assembly, there will be many occasions in life when they will need to be patient and therefore patience is a valuable personal quality for them to develop.

Related assemblies None

Poacher turned gamekeeper

Theme   Changing character for the better

Date   No specific date

Materials
- OHP and screen
- OHP 1 Poacher turned gamekeeper (page 66)
- OHP 2 Turn over a new leaf (page 67)
- OHP 3 Make a fresh start (page 68)
- Blank card for covering parts of the OHP pictures

Assembly organization   Start the assembly by explaining that you want to play a game with them in which they will have to guess the words of a common saying from a picture.

Put OHP 1 on the screen. (Most of the picture should be covered.)

Show the partly covered picture and ask the pupils if they can guess what the saying is. Continue by revealing more of the picture until the pupils guess the saying. (For younger pupils the saying could be provided on a large sheet of paper and they merely have to match the picture with the right saying.)

Once the saying has been worked out, take a few minutes to explain its meaning, including the fact that the saying involves having the chance to change their behaviour for the better.

Repeat the process above for OHPs 2 and 3. After working through each saying ask the pupils what the three sayings have in common. Bring out the answer: Making a change for the better. Go on to explain that we all have faults in our character or behaviour that we should change. Illustrate this with the saying 'Nobody's perfect' and explain its meaning.

Ask the pupils to give examples of types of behaviour which are unacceptable and therefore need to be changed or avoided. Some examples you might like to bring out are:

- bullying
- laziness
- big-headedness
- untidiness
- name-calling
- unreliability

Go on to explain that once you realize that there is something about you or your behaviour that people do not like or find unacceptable, you need to remember the three sayings the assembly started with and make a change for the better.

If you wish, you could illustrate this idea of people having faults in their character and needing to change their ways by telling them the story of Matthew the tax collector who Jesus called to become one of his followers (Matthew 9: 9–13).

Conclude the assembly by saying that of course you are talking of changes for the better. You don't want to hear of a person turning over a new leaf and becoming a bully.

Related assembly   The writing is on the wall

Crime and punishment

Theme What is wrong is wrong

Date No specific date

Materials None

Before the assembly you will need to ask six volunteers to practise the courtroom scenes shown below. They will play the following parts

> Two judges (one male, one female)
> Two clerks
> First accused (Mrs Smith)
> Second accused (Mr Jones)

Assembly organization Start the assembly by explaining to the pupils that you want them to watch two short plays. The first four volunteers should already be seated at the front of the assembly. Introduce the first play to the pupils by pointing out that they will see the end of a trial in which an accused woman is told the verdict and sentenced for a series of crimes.

Play 1 **Clerk 1** Will the accused please stand and face the judge.
Mrs Smith stands and faces Judge 1.

Judge 1 For the theft of £2000 from a local fruit shop, you have been found guilty – I sentence you to four years in prison.

For the theft of £400 from a local pensioner, you have been found guilty – I sentence you to one year in prison.

For the theft of £20,000 from a local bank, you have been found guilty – I sentence you to ten years in prison.

For the theft of £30,000 from a local building society, you have been found guilty – I sentence you to ten years in prison.

Next introduce to the assembly the second play, in which an accused man is told the verdict and sentenced. While you talk, your volunteers should get into their starting positions.

Play 2 **Clerk 2** Will the accused please stand and face the judge.
Mr Jones stands and faces Judge 2.

Judge 2 For the theft of £52,400 worth of jewellery from a local jewellers, you have been found guilty – I sentence you to twenty-five years in prison.

Go on to explain that the two plays represent imaginary crimes and sentences and that you would like to look at each in a little more detail.

Point out that in Play 1 Mrs Smith had committed a series of crimes (some of which were relatively minor). Ask the pupils how much in total she had stolen. (It might be useful to go back and remind the pupils of the four crimes and the amounts stolen.) Bring out the answer: £52,400. Ask the pupils how long she was sentenced to prison for her crimes. Bring out the answer: 25 years.

Then go on to point out that in Play 2 Mr Jones had committed one large crime. Ask the pupils how much he had stolen. Bring out the answer: £52,400. Ask the pupils how long he was sentenced to prison for his crime. Bring out the answer: 25 years.

Ask the pupils what do they notice about the amounts of money stolen and the length of the prison sentences given to both Mrs Smith and Mr Jones. Bring out the answer: They stole the same amount of money and were sentenced to prison for the same length of time. (You might like to point out that although the crimes and sentences in these plays are imaginary, it can be true that people who commit lots of minor crimes in the end spend as much of their lives in prison as someone who commits one major crime).

Go on to point out that these two plays illustrate the point that there are no degrees of right or wrong, something cannot be just a little bit wrong. If you wish you could demonstrate this idea by pointing out that a person who steals £10 from a shop has done wrong, just as a person who steals £100 from a shop has done wrong. This could be related to the eighth commandment (Exodus 20: 1–17): You should not steal. It does not say: You should not steal large amounts of money, or You should not steal from poor people but it's OK to steal from the wealthy.

Conclude the assembly by reminding the pupils that it is the action of stealing which is wrong, no matter how much is taken, and that this is true for all wrong-doings. They cannot be qualified to become something that is less wrong or even something which is right. What is wrong is wrong and you should not do it for any reason.

Related assemblies None

The devil finds work

Theme   Making good use of your time

Date   No specific date

Materials
- Items that illustrate the hobbies you wish to talk about. (Try not to give a sexist bias to the hobbies covered.) Some examples might be:

a football	a book	a frying pan
a pair of knitting needles	a hockey stick	a basketball
a saw	a spade	a paintbrush

Before the assembly arrange for two or three volunteers to prepare a brief talk on one of their interests.

Assembly organization
Start the assembly by gathering at the front enough pupils to demonstrate the hobbies you wish to illustrate. Give each of the pupils you have at the front one of the hobby items you have chosen. (Tell any pupils that are given a ball not to throw or kick it.) An element of fun can be introduced if the pupils are given the names of the items to mime instead of the actual items to demonstrate.

Ask the pupils what connection there could be between the various items or actions being demonstrated. Bring out the answer: They are all examples of things that people use or do in their hobbies. Go on to talk about each of the items and the part they play in people's hobbies. The following points relate to the items listed above:

Football
Ask the pupils how many of them play football. Point out to them that playing football not only helps to keep them fit and healthy, but is also a sensible way to use up some of their spare time. (These points can be made in relation to any sport.)

Knitting needles
Ask the pupils how many of them know how to knit. Explain to the assembly that not only does knitting provide them with a useful pastime, it can also save them money as they can make some of their own clothes.

Saw
Ask the assembly how many of their parents do repair jobs around the house. Point out that many adults do their own repair jobs as part of their hobby. Some of them become very good at it and can save themselves a great deal of money.

Books
Ask how many of the pupils have magazines they read regularly. Ask how many of them have read a book at home in the last

month. Point out that not only is reading a useful and enjoyable way to spend your time, it also helps to increase your knowledge and improve your reading.

Frying pan Ask the pupils how many of them know how to cook a simple meal (e.g. beans on toast). Go on to explain that when they get older they will all need to be able to cook a few meals. When they leave home they will not be able to live on beans on toast.

Spade Ask the assembly how many of their parents do their own gardening. (Not just cutting the grass, but also growing flowers and even vegetables.) Explain that gardening is another productive hobby, as you can grow your own food and save yourself a lot of money.

Conclude this part of the assembly by asking your volunteers to deliver their talks on their interests.

Next ask the assembly if any of them have heard of the saying 'The devil finds work for idle hands'. Ask them what they think this means. Bring out the answer: If you have nothing to do, you will get bored and then get into trouble doing something you should not, just to relieve the boredom.

Conclude the assembly by pointing out that one way to avoid becoming bored and to stop yourself from getting into trouble is to ensure you have a number of hobbies which can fill up your time usefully and keep you out of trouble.

Related assemblies None

Heads you win

Theme   The danger of gambling

Date   No specific date

Materials
- Two coins
- Three sets of six fruit pictures on card (These can be copied and cut out from page 75)

Assembly organization   Start the assembly by flipping a coin and asking if anyone can tell you whether it is heads or tails. Repeat this two or three times asking different pupils to guess whether it is heads or tails. (Continue until a few pupils have guessed correctly.) Next ask the pupils what we would call this if we started to bet money on the result? Bring out the answer: Gambling.

Move on to talk about how easy it seems to be to win if all you have to do is guess whether it is heads or tails. (Mention how many of them guessed correctly.) Go on to ask the assembly if they can tell you what the chances were that you would get the answer correct. Bring out the answer: One chance in two.

Explain to the pupils that the coin has two sides and that you pick one of those, giving you a one-in-two chance of being correct. Continue by explaining that gambling is never as simple as this; you always have a lower than one-in-two chance of winning. If you wish you could emphasize this point by repeating the coin-flipping exercise using two coins. This time, you can tell the pupils they will only have a one-in-four chance of predicting correctly. Explain to the assembly that you want to go on and look at a more realistic gambling situation.

Call three volunteers to the front, and give each one a set of the six fruit cards. Explain to the pupils that when they are told to start, the volunteers will shuffle the cards until they are told to stop. When they stop, the volunteers will hold up the top card.

Ask the assembly which form of gambling this represents. Bring out the answer: Fruit machines. Ask a pupil to predict the three fruits that will be on top when the volunteers stop shuffling. Then ask the volunteers to start shuffling. Allow the pupil who made the prediction to stop the shuffling. See if his/her prediction is correct. Repeat the process a number of times with different pupils making predictions.

When the exercise is finished explain what chance the pupils had of getting their predictions correct – 1 in 216. (Each pile has six cards and there are three piles. This means there are 216 ($6 \times 6 \times 6$) different results of which only one is correct). Go on to explain that proper fruit machines have many more than six symbols on each wheel; this means that although there are more winning combinations, the chances of winning remain small. If we imagine the machine has ten symbols on each wheel, the chances of winning the jackpot are 1 in 1000.

Next pose the question that if people have such small chances of winning, why do they carry on playing the fruit machines? Is it because of the excitement they get wondering if they will win and the hope that by spending just a little more money, they could win the jackpot? Suggest that it is the excitement of gambling that causes the problem, because it can make gambling addictive (which means you cannot stop yourself from doing it).

Many people waste a great deal of their hard earned money on various forms of gambling and can even get themselves into a great deal of debt.

If you wish you could also mention that a report issued in 1995 suggested that people with very little money were spending money they needed for food on National Lottery tickets.

Ask the assembly if they know the name of the group which people can join if they become addicted to gambling. Bring out the answer: Gamblers Anonymous.

Conclude the assembly by reminding the pupils of the saying 'You don't get anything for nothing', and that when people do win at gambling they often win much less than they have already paid out.

Related assemblies None

APPLE

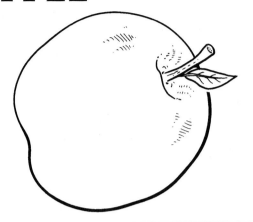

CHERRIES

PEAR

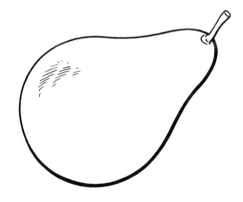

ORANGE

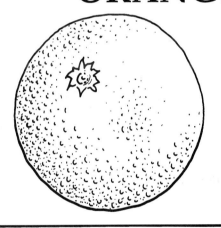

BANANA

GRAPES

Pride comes before a fall

Theme   Taking pride in what you do

Date   No specific date

Materials
- Five large sheets of paper, each with one of the following words written on it in large letters: Pride comes before a fall
- Three large sheets of paper, each with one of the following possible meanings of the word 'pride' written on it in large letters:
  Feeling pleased with something you have done
  Stubborn feeling which won't allow you to change your mind
  A collection of lions

Assembly organization

Start the assembly by asking for five volunteers to come to the front and give them one word each from the five-word saying above. Arrange them so that they are in the correct order, but do not let them show the words to the rest of the pupils at this stage.

Explain to the assembly that today you want to look at the meaning of a saying in which the key word is 'pride'. Ask the pupil holding the word pride to show it to the rest of the assembly. Go on to ask the assembly if they can tell you some meanings of this word.

Now ask three volunteers to come to the front and give each of them one of the meanings of the word you have prepared, again asking them not to show the meanings just yet. Bring out from the assembly the three meanings you have written on the sheets of paper. As they give you each definition ask the volunteer holding it to turn their sheet round and show the rest of the pupils the meaning.

Draw the pupils' attention back to the original saying (of which only the word pride is shown) and ask them if they know the rest of the saying. (If you wish you could ask a member of staff to complete the saying.) Bring out the answer: Pride comes before a fall. At this point ask your volunteers to turn the rest of the words round to show the assembly the full saying. If you wish you could relate this saying to a similar one found in the Bible (Proverbs 16, 18).

Ask the pupils which of the three meanings of pride would definitely not refer to the saying. Bring out the answer: A pride of lions. Go on to ask the assembly which of the remaining two meanings of the word pride could result in you having a fall (you might also like to explain that the saying does not mean a fall in that you fall over, but that things go wrong.) Bring out the answer: Stubborn feeling which won't allow you to change your mind.

Next talk to the pupils about some of the ways in which pride could result in a fall (things going wrong). For example: You cannot find your way on a map, and your pride will not let you admit that you are lost and seek help, so you continue to go the wrong way. Or, you have had an argument with a friend, and your pride will not let you admit you were wrong, so you fall out with your friend.

Conclude the assembly by reminding the pupils that they should take pride in their work and that having pride in what you do is a good thing. However, they should avoid stubborn pride which won't allow them to admit when they are in the wrong. It is much better to be able to admit when you are in the wrong and be able to change your mind.

Related assemblies None

Fools rush in

Theme   The importance of thinking before you act

Date   No specific date

Materials   • Two pieces of paper, each with one of the following words
                    written on it in large letters:
                    Understanding
                    Knowledge

Assembly organization   Start the assembly by telling the pupils that you want them to
                    imagine they are about to buy a new house. Ask them if they
                    think this is an easy thing, like going into a shop to buy a bag of
                    sweets. Bring out the answer: No.
                         Go on to explain that you are going to tell them about the
                    work two different builders offer to do and how much it will cost.
                    They have to decide which builder they would like to build their
                    new house for them.

Builder 1   This company offers to build you a very nice house and has
                    found a beautiful location on a sandy beach by a lake. They can
                    build the house in four months and will charge you £20,000.

Builder 2   This company offers to build you an equally nice house at exactly
                    the same location, but they say it will take them two months to
                    find the best site where the foundations are strong enough to
                    build your house. This means that it will take them six months to
                    build the house and it will cost you £26,000.
                         Ask the pupils for a show of hands to vote for the builder
                    they would choose to build their house. Count how many votes
                    each builder gets and talk to the children about why they chose
                    Builder 2. If the majority did not choose Builder 2 you will have
                    to explain why it would be the best company. Some points to
                    bring out would be:

• Builder 1 was going to build the house on poor foundations; it
  would soon collapse.
• Builder 2 was obviously going to take care to find the correct
  place to build a house that would last.
• Builder 1 would be cheaper but the house might not be as
  good as cheaper materials may have been used.
• Builder 2 would be more expensive but would probably build a
  better house.

Explain to the assembly that this story reminds you of the saying
'Fools rush in where angels fear to tread'. You can explain that

this means that fools rush into something where sensible people take the time to think about it and make a wise decision. Go on to talk to the pupils about what they should do as sensible people (and not fools) to help them make wise decisions.

Bring out the following ideas:

- You must get to know everything you can about the decision you have to make. (Ask for a volunteer to come forward and to hold up the sign saying 'Knowledge'.)
- You must understand the consequences of any decisions you make. (Ask for a volunteer to come forward and to hold up the sign saying 'Understanding'.)

Next, explain that common to the story of the builders and the saying is the idea that you must take care in making decisions. Conclude this part of the assembly by looking at the implications of this idea in two possible situations which the pupils could actually be faced with:

1 Someone tells you that a person is saying unpleasant things about you.
   Do not go straight over to the other person and accuse them of saying things about you; they may not have said a thing. Someone may just be setting you up to do the wrong thing in anger.
2 You are told by a friend that they have seen someone in your class using the pen that you lost yesterday.
   Do not go over and accuse the person of stealing your pen; they may have bought exactly the same pen as you.

Conclude the assembly by asking the pupils where the original story of the two builders comes from. Bring out the answer: The parable of the two house builders told by Jesus (Matthew 7: 24–27). You might like then to finish by talking about the meaning behind the original parable.

Related assembly   King Canute

Bible stories

These assemblies take stories from the Bible and relate them to modern-day life, while still providing the chance to tell the story with its original meaning.

Assembly	Theme
John's red Ferrari	*Jealousy*
Noah's Ark	*Positive personal qualities*
Jonah and the whale	*Positive personal qualities*
The giant-killer	*Determination, hard work and self-confidence*
Into the lions' den	*Having the courage to do what you know is right*
The writing is on the wall	*Changing character for the better*

John's red Ferrari

Theme Jealousy

Date No specific date

Materials None

Assembly organization Start the assembly by telling the pupils that you want them to listen to the following story:

- There once was a rich farmer who had twelve sons, the youngest of whom was called John. He was the farmer's favourite.
- One day the farmer gave John a red Ferrari. The other brothers were very jealous of their father's gift to their younger brother. It made them extremely angry and they were very nasty to John, calling him names. They did not have a kind word to say about him.
- John didn't help the situation because he started to tell his brothers about the dreams he was having. In one dream the brothers were all racing cars around the farm and John, in his red Ferrari, won every time. In another dream John was racing his red Ferrari in the Le Mans 24-hour race, which he won. In the crowd, cheering with everyone else, were his mother, father and brothers.
- These dreams made the brothers even angrier and even John's father told him off, although he did wonder if perhaps the dreams might come true one day.
- At this time John's brothers had to go to another country on business for their father. As they went the brothers started to plan how they could get rid of their little brother. After the brothers had left, their father noticed that they had left behind some of the money and travellers cheques they would need for their food and accommodation. He sent John in his red Ferrari to catch them up and give them the money.
- When John caught up with his brothers they took the opportunity to put an end to his good fortune, but they did not want to hurt him. So they framed him with causing a serious car crash, for which he was arrested and sent to prison. They also pushed his car off a high cliff causing it to explode. They then took pictures of the wrecked car.
- When they returned home the brothers told their father that John had been killed in a serious car accident and that his body had been burnt beyond recognition. They showed him the pictures of the car crash as evidence and said that they had arranged for their brother's body to be buried.

Having told the assembly this story ask them which emotion John's brothers had shown that had caused them to be so unkind to him. Bring out the answer: Jealousy. Go on to explain that jealousy over other people's belongings or their lifestyle can cause many problems:

- You may be unpleasant to someone because you are jealous of the things they have.
- You may vandalize someone's belongings because you are jealous of what they have.
- You may be tempted to steal someone's belongings because you are jealous of what they have.

Go on to point out to the pupils that jealousy is a very destructive emotion and that instead of being jealous of other people they should be thankful for what they have.

At this point you could ask the pupils if they can tell you where the story you told them originally came from. Bring out the answer: The story of Joseph and his brothers from the Bible (Genesis 37: 1–36).

Conclude the assembly by reminding the pupils that jealousy is a very destructive emotion, which can cause people to do very unpleasant things. Joseph's brothers' jealousy meant they were very unpleasant to him and even sold him as a slave to be taken away to another land where they would never see him again.

Related assemblies None

Noah's Ark

Theme   Positive personal qualities

Date   At the start of the school year

Materials
- OHP and screen
- OHP 1 Noah's Ark (page 85)
- Set of OHP pens
- Six large sheets of paper, each with one of the following six names on one side and a number (1 to 6) on the other:

| God | Ark | Mount Ararat |
| Noah | animals | dove |

Assembly organization   Start the assembly by explaining to the pupils that you want them to take part in a little quiz on a famous story from the Bible. Ask for six volunteers to come up to the front, and give each of them one of the sheets of paper you have prepared to hold up so that the name is showing.

Ask the assembly if they can tell you the name of the story that is indicated by the words shown. Bring out the answer: Noah's Ark. Go on to explain that you are going to read out six questions and that they have to pick the correct answer from the names shown at the front. Before reading out the questions ask the volunteers to turn round their sheets of paper (to show only the numbers) and to swap places with each other. This turns the quiz into a memory exercise.

Read out the following six questions in order, one after the other. After each question ask the pupils in the assembly to try and pick the correct answer using the numbers.

1 Who sent the rain?
2 Who built the boat?
3 What was the boat called?
4 What went into the boat in twos?
5 Where did the boat finally come to rest after the rains?
6 Which bird came back with a twig?

When a wrong answer is picked the volunteer should turn their paper back round to show the number. If the answer is correct the volunteer should continue to display the correct answer until all the questions have been answered.

Continue asking the series of questions in the same order until all the correct answers have been found. Once this has been achieved put the names back into the correct order and briefly remind the pupils of the story of Noah's Ark (Genesis 6, 7, 8, 9).

Next go on to ask the pupils why, in this story, God decided to flood the Earth and destroy all the humans except Noah and his family. Bring out the answer: All the humans were unkind and violent. (You will need to have made sure this answer was covered in your brief summary above.)

Point out to the assembly that today you want to show them how at the start of a new school year they have the chance to get rid of all their bad habits. In the story from the Bible God removed all the violence and unkindness on the Earth. In a similar way they must develop during the next year only the good habits shown by Noah and his family.

Put OHP 1 on the screen.

Explain to the assembly that you want them to tell you which are the good qualities they should develop and which are the bad ones they should avoid. Bring out a list of positive qualities, which can be written in the Ark to be 'saved', and a list of negative ones, which can be written in the sea to be 'destroyed'. Some examples might be:

- hardworking/lazy
- tidy/untidy
- polite/rude
- reliable/unreliable
- helpful/unhelpful
- honest/dishonest
- kind/unkind

Conclude the assembly by talking about the positive qualities contained inside the Ark as being the ones for them to develop over the next year (if they haven't already done so!).

Related assembly   Jonah and the whale

Jonah and the whale

Theme   Positive personal qualities

Date   No specific date

Materials
- Six sheets of paper, each with one of the following pairs of words written in large letters on either side of the sheet:

    gentle/violent
    kind/cruel
    polite/rude
    passive/aggressive
    honest/dishonest
    tolerant/intolerant

Assembly organization   Start the assembly by asking the pupils to listen to a series of six questions. After each question ask if anyone would like to try and guess the name of the person in the story.

1 Who caught a ship from Joppa?
2 Who was trying to get to Tarshish?
3 Who should have gone to Nineveh?
4 Who was at sea during a storm?
5 Who was thrown overboard by the crew?
6 Who was swallowed by a whale?

Once the pupils have guessed that the name of the character is Jonah, go on to explain a little more about the story of Jonah and the whale (Jonah 1, 2, 3). Some points you might like to mention are:

- God chose Jonah to carry a message to the people of Nineveh.
- God told Jonah to go and tell the people of Nineveh that they must change their wicked ways or God would destroy their city.
- Jonah did not like the idea of going to Nineveh as its people were cruel and enemies of the Israelites (Jonah was an Israelite).
- Instead Jonah went to Joppa and set sail on a ship bound for Tarshish in Spain.
- Once at sea the ship was caught in a terrible storm.
- Jonah told the crew that it was God that had sent the storm because he had disobeyed Him.
- Jonah told the crew that if they threw him overboard the storm might stop – which they did and the storm did stop.
- Afraid he would drown, Jonah prayed for God to help him.

God sent a whale to swallow Jonah.

- While inside the whale Jonah realized God had saved him and how silly he had been to disobey God.
- Jonah made up his mind that if he survived he would go to Nineveh.
- After three days and nights the whale spat Jonah out onto the seashore and God said to Jonah that he was being given a second chance to take his message to Nineveh.
- When Jonah told the people of Nineveh God's message, they changed their behaviour and abandoned their wicked ways.
- God saw what the people of Nineveh had done and forgave them for all their wickedness.

Go on to explain to the assembly that one of the things this story tells us is that we should not behave badly. However, we still need to know which ways of behaving are wrong so that we can avoid behaving in those ways.

Ask for six volunteers to come to the front of the assembly. Give each of them one of the sheets of paper so that the six unacceptable ways of behaving are shown to the assembly. Go on to talk about these as being examples of unacceptable ways of behaving that we should avoid. (As you talk about each one ask the pupil holding that sign to step forward.) Some points you might like to bring out about each of these ways of behaving are:

- Violent – bullies who use violence or people who try to deal with situations using violence.
- Cruel – those who take delight in being unpleasant or nasty to others.
- Rude – being impolite or having no manners.
- Aggressive – using physical or verbal violence.
- Dishonest – being unable to be trusted by others.
- Intolerant – not being prepared to accept the beliefs or ideas of others.

Having talked about these examples as being the sort of bad behaviour that is unacceptable and the way we should not behave, conclude the assembly by asking the pupils at the front to turn their sheets of paper round to show the positive qualities. Explain to the assembly that these are the types of acceptable behaviour they should be developing as they go through school and life.

Related assembly   Noah's Ark

The giant-killer

Theme   Determination, hard work and self-confidence

Date   No specific date

Materials   None

Assembly organization   Start the assembly by talking to the pupils about an imaginary sporting event (of your own choice) in which a very successful and talented team or player plays against an unknown team or player. For example: Manchester United playing Grimsby Town in an FA Cup match. Ask the pupils who they would expect to win. Bring out the answer: The most talented team or player.

Go on to explain that there are occasions when the unknown team or player can win and when this happens the unexpected winners are often called 'giant-killers'. (This part of the assembly could be given more relevance by referring to an actual recent sporting event of this type.)

Ask the pupils what qualities the unknown team or player must have if they are to beat the more successful team (or, if there is a real-life example, what qualities the winners had). Some examples to bring out might be:

- hard work
- determination
- confidence

Conclude this part of the assembly by saying that people can achieve the unexpected when they try hard enough.

Go on to ask the pupils what the origin of the term 'giant-killer' might be. Bring out the answer: The killing of the giant Goliath by David. Tell the assembly the story of David and Goliath (1 Samuel: 17). You might like to mention some of the following points:

- David brought his brothers, who were soldiers in the Israelite army, some food.
- He found that his brothers and all the Israelites were frightened of the Philistine army because of the giant Goliath.
- Goliath came forward and roared for one of the Israelites to come out and fight him.
- David volunteered to go forward and fight Goliath as he was sure God was on his side.
- David went forward to fight Goliath armed only with his sling and a few stones.

- Goliath made fun of David, but David killed him with his sling and a single stone.
- The Philistine army were so terrified at the death of Goliath that they fled and were defeated by the Israelites.

If you wish, you could ask the pupils what helped David have the confidence to go forward, fight and kill Goliath. Some answers to bring out might be:

- courage
- skilfulness with his sling shot
- faith in God

Conclude the assembly by reminding the pupils that as in the case of today's 'giant-killers' in sports, they too can achieve great things with hard work, determination and a little self-confidence.

Related assemblies None

Into the lions' den

Theme   Having the courage to do what you know is right

Date   No specific date

Materials   ● A chair for Nebuchadnezzar and (later) Darius to sit on

Before the assembly you will need to work with a group of pupils to practise their parts in the following mini-play.

Assembly organization   Start the assembly by asking the pupils if any of them have heard of the saying 'Into the lions' den'. Ask them what they think the saying means. Bring out the answer: Going into a situation where everyone is against you, where everyone disagrees with you.

Next ask the pupils if they can tell you where the saying comes from. Bring out the answer: The Bible story of Daniel being put into the lions' den (Daniel 6: 1–28).

Ask your group of volunteers to act out the following mini-play.

Narrator   Here we see Daniel and the Jewish people being led away into slavery.

   ○ *A group of pupils mime being tied together, walking in a line, heads bowed, hands held together behind their backs. Another group of pupils walk alongside these and in front of them, miming whipping them along.*

Narrator   When the Jewish people arrived in Babylon, King Nebuchadnezzar ordered his officials to select some of the prisoners to serve in the court.

   ○ *Nebuchadnezzar, seated and surrounded by his officials, sends one official over to select servants. One of the officials walks over to the prisoners and takes Daniel out to stand by Nebuchadnezzar. The other prisoners and guards walk off and sit out of the way.*

Narrator   Daniel became one of Nebuchadnezzar's most trusted advisors

   ○ *Daniel, standing at Nebuchadnezzar's side, points to a document Nebuchadnezzar is miming reading.*

Narrator   After many years Nebuchadnezzar died. Eventually Darius became king.

   ○ *Officials surrounding Nebuchadnezzar pick him up from his chair and carry him away. Darius enters and sits in Nebuchadnezzar's chair.*

Narrator   Darius realized Daniel was an honest and trustworthy man so he placed him in charge of his officials.

> ○   *Darius mimes looking at a document. Daniel, standing by his side, mimes pointing out parts of the document.*

Narrator   Darius's advisors were jealous of Daniel so they convinced Darius to sign a law banning anyone praying to any God, other than King Darius. Daniel's principles would not let him obey this law and he was thrown into the lions' den as a punishment.

Ask the assembly what happened to Daniel in the lions' den. Bring out the answer: God sent down an angel and closed the lions' mouths, so Daniel survived.

Go on to point out that this story of Daniel being thrown into the lions' den is the origin of the saying you started the assembly with. It is used when a person is faced with a situation where it is necessary to do what they know is correct despite the possible consequences. Finally talk to the pupils about situations where they may need to 'go into the lions' den' and do what they know is right even though everyone else may be trying to get them to do otherwise. Some examples might be:

- Having to walk away from someone who is trying to provoke you into a fight, even if everyone else is calling you 'chicken'.
- Not stealing something from a shop, even if all your friends are encouraging you to do so.
- Not trying a cigarette (or drugs) even if your best friend is encouraging you to do so.

Conclude the assembly by reminding the pupils that having the courage to do what they think is right will never literally get them put into the lions' den, but there are many situations when it is necessary for us to stand up for what we know is right, no matter what the cost.

Related assembly   Edith Cavell

The writing is on the wall

Theme   Changing character for the better

Date   No specific date

Materials
- A large sheet of paper with the following saying written on it in large letters:
  The writing is on the wall
- Four sheets of paper, each with one of the following words written on it in large letters:
  mene   mene   tekel   upharsin

Assembly organization

Start the assembly by asking one volunteer to come forward and hold up your saying while you read it to the assembly. Point out to the pupils that this saying comes from a story in the Bible (Daniel 5: 1–31). Go on to explain a little of the story of Daniel interpreting the writing. Some points you might like to make are:

- After the death of Nebuchadnezzar, his son Belshazzar became king.
- Belshazzar held a great feast at which he and his guests gave thanks to the gods of gold, silver, brass and others.
- At this time a hand appeared which Belshazzar saw and it started to write on the wall.

(Ask four more volunteers to come to the front and hold up the four words on separate sheets of paper.)

- The hand started to write the words:
  mene   mene   tekel   upharsin
- The king sent for his wise men to translate the meaning of the writing, but none of them could understand it.
- The queen mother told Belshazzar that a man called Daniel would be able to translate the writing.
- Daniel was sent for and he translated the writing.
  mene – God has judged your kingdom and finished it.
  tekel – You have been weighed on the scales and found to be lacking.
  upharsin – Your kingdom will be divided and given to the Medes and the Persians.
- That night Belshazzar was killed and Darius took over his kingdom.

Relate the story back to your original saying and explain to the assembly that when the saying is used today, it does not literally mean that a hand is writing on the wall, but that something is obviously going to happen because, for example, of the way a person is behaving.

Further illustrate this point by talking about an imaginary pupil who is not working hard in lessons and how the saying 'the writing is on the wall' could apply to this individual in the sense that his/her lack of effort indicates an obvious lack of future success.

Go on to explain that in this and many other cases where a pupil's work or behaviour is not as would be desired, it is not necessary for 'the writing to be on the wall' – in other words, their future is not decided. It is possible for them to 'turn over a new leaf', to see where they are going wrong and to change their ways.

Conclude the assembly by suggesting that the pupils should look at their work and behaviour to see if 'the writing is on the wall' in any areas of their life. If it appears to be, they should think about making the necessary changes, as it is not too late for them to improve and make a success of their future.

Related assembly Poacher turned gamekeeper

Saints

These assemblies provide an opportunity to look at the life of, or legends behind, a number of the saints. At the start of whichever assembly you use first it might be worthwhile explaining to the pupils what is meant by a saint. A suitable explanation would be: a person who has been recognized by the Church as being a very holy person and who it is believed God has given a high place in heaven.

Assembly	Theme
Peter (the rock)	*St Peter*
Forty days of rain	*St Swithin*
St Hilda	*Female saints (St Hilda)*
Patron saint of travellers	*St Christopher*
Doubting Thomas	*St Thomas*
Paul's journey	*St Paul*

Peter (the rock)

Theme St Peter

Date On or near 29 June

Materials
- Seven sheets of paper, each with one of the following statements written on it:
  He was a fisherman.
  Originally he was called Simon.
  He was one of Jesus's twelve disciples.
  Jesus described him as 'the rock' upon which the church would be built.
  He is claimed to have been the first pope.
  His body is believed to be buried inside the walls of the Vatican City.
  He is the patron saint of fishermen.

Before the assembly select seven volunteers from your form and allow them time to practise reading the above statements.

Assembly organization Start the assembly by explaining to the pupils that you want them to listen to a series of seven sentences about a famous man. When they have listened to them all ask whether someone would like to tell you who the sentences describe.

Ask your volunteers to read their sentences one at a time in the above order. Then ask the assembly who the man was. Bring out the answer: St Peter. Go back to each of the statements and give the pupils a little more information about each one.

- St Peter lived with his brother Andrew (St Andrew) and his family near Lake Galilee, where they made their living as fishermen. At that time he was called Simon. At their first meeting Jesus gave Peter the name Cephas, which translates into Peter and means 'a rock' (John 1: 40–42).
- While walking by Lake Galilee Jesus saw Peter and his brother fishing; he said to them, 'Come with me and I will teach you to catch people.' At once they left their nets and went with Jesus (Matthew 4: 18–20).
- Jesus went with his disciples to the town of Caesarea Philippi. While talking to them, Jesus said to Peter, 'You are a rock, and on this rock foundation I will build my church' (Matthew 16: 13–20).
- Roman Catholics believe the Pope is the successor of St Peter, who Jesus described as the rock upon which the church would be built. This is called the apostolic succession.

- The first Christian church in Rome – the Basilica of Constantine – was built on the site where the emperor Nero had Christians crucified. St Peter was crucified there in AD 67 and buried somewhere nearby. In fact many Christians believe that St Peter's body is buried under the altar of the church that stands on the spot now – the Basilica of St Peter. (Bones excavated in 1968 were accepted by Pope Paul VI as those of St Peter.)
- Probably because of his early life as a fisherman, St Peter was taken as the patron saint of fishermen.

Conclude the assembly by pointing out to the pupils that St Peter's feast day is 29 June and that on that day they might like to remember St Peter and some of the events of his life.

Related assemblies None

Forty days of rain

Theme St Swithin

Date In the Summer term (as near as possible to 15 July)

Materials
- OHP and screen
- OHP 1 map of Britain (page 99)
- Set of OHP pens

Assembly organization Put OHP 1 on the screen.

Start the assembly by explaining that as it will soon be the start of the summer holidays, you would like to start today's assembly with a long-range weather forecast you have managed to get. Point to the date shown on the screen and explain that the forecast is for 15 July and from that you can tell what the weather will be like for most of the summer.

Point to a number of areas of the country (including your own local area), predict either rain or dry weather and draw the appropriate symbol on the map.

Next ask the assembly if anyone can predict what the weather will be like for the following 40 days from 15 July in the areas you have predicted rain. Bring out the answer: It should rain. Repeat the question for the areas where you have predicted dry weather. Bring out the answer: It should be dry.

Next go on to explain that these predictions are based on the old story which says that if it rains on 15 July, which is called St Swithin's Day, it will rain for the next 40 days.

For the next part of the assembly go on to explain a few facts about St Swithin. Some examples might be:

- St Swithin was born in an area of England called Wessex in the 9th century and lived in the town of Winchester. (Show the pupils where Winchester is on the map of Britain.)
- He became adviser to King Egbert and taught Egbert's son Ethelwolf, who made him Bishop of Winchester.
- St Swithin was a good, kind man, famous for his charitable gifts and for building many churches.
- When he died in AD 862 St Swithin was buried (as he requested) in a common site outside the cathedral. Many years later when monks moved his body into the cathedral it started to rain and it carried on raining for forty days. The monks took the rain as being a sign of St Swithin's disapproval of being moved. This rain, when his body was moved, and a number of

miracle cures that occurred at the same time were considered to be signs of St Swithin's saintly powers.

This is one explanation for the belief that if it rains on St Swithin's Day, it will rain for the next 40 days – which is the origin of the saying:

St Swithin's day, if thou dost rain,
For forty days it will rain
St Swithin's Day, if thou be fair
For forty days t'will rain no more.

Conclude the assembly by reminding the pupils that 15 July is St Swithin's Day and that, according to the old story, on that day you can tell the weather for the next 40 days.

Related assemblies None

15 July

Winchester

St Hilda

Theme Female saints (St Hilda)

Date On or near 17 November

Materials • Eight sheets of paper, each with one of the following names written on it in large letters:
Andrew
David
George
Patrick
Valentine
Nicholas
Christopher
Peter

Assembly organization Start the assembly by asking eight volunteers to come to the front and hold up their sheets of paper. Then ask the assembly what these names have in common. Bring out the answer: They are all saints.

Go on to ask the pupils what other group of names they can see that have something in common. Bring out the answer: George, Andrew, David, Patrick. Ask the pupils what these names have in common. Bring out the answer: They are the patron saints of England, Scotland, Wales and Ireland.

If you wish you could next ask the pupils to tell you which of these countries has which patron saints.

England – George
Scotland – Andrew
Wales – David
Ireland – Patrick

Go back and remind the assembly that these people are all saints and that they must have lived a very Christian life. That fact was recognized when the Church named them as saints.

Ask the pupils what else all these names have in common. Bring out the answer: They are all men. Go on to point out that it has not only been men who have shown the qualities worthy of sainthood; there are many women who have been made saints. Tell the assembly that today you are going to talk about an important English female Saint called St Hilda.

Some facts about St Hilda that you might like to point out are:

- She was born in AD 614 (over 1000 years ago) and began her life as an English princess. (Her uncle was King Edwin of Northumbria.) Both Hilda and her uncle Edwin were baptised together by Paulinus, a monk and Bishop of York.
- At the age of 33 Hilda became a nun and in AD 657 she founded (or possibly refounded) an abbey in Whitby (which is on the North Sea coast in Yorkshire) of which she was abbess.
- During the years she presided over the abbey, Hilda taught people about the gospel of Jesus and helped them to lead good and useful lives.
- She developed a reputation for wisdom and being available to talk to anyone. For this reason she was asked to give advice not only to common people but also to kings.
- Because of her compassion and charity she became known as 'Mother Hilda'.
- She was also known for her enthusiasm towards learning. She established many libraries and encouraged the work of the Anglo-Saxon poet Caedman, who looked after the Abbey's cattle.
- During the last six years of her life Hilda carried on her work in spite of a very serious illness and great pain. According to one story, the last words she said were to remember the words of St Matthew: 'Happy are those who work for peace; God will call them his children' (Matthew 5: 9).
- Hilda finally died on 17 November AD 680.

Go on to ask the assembly if any of them can guess on what day St Hilda's feast day is celebrated. Bring out the answer: 17 November.

Conclude the assembly by reminding the pupils that on 17 November they might like to remember that it is St Hilda's feast day and to think of the facts you have told them about her life.

Related assemblies None

Patron saint of travellers

Theme   St Christopher

Date   Towards the end of the Summer term

Materials
- OHP and screen
- OHP 1 St Christopher (page 104)
- St Christopher medallion

Assembly organization   Start the assembly by explaining that you want the pupils to look closely at a picture.

Put OHP 1 on the screen.

Ask the assembly if they can tell you the name of the character represented in the picture. Bring out the answer: St Christopher. (To help younger pupils, you might like to show them the medallion as a clue.) Next go on to talk about the things they notice in the picture. Some points to bring out are:

- In the centre there is a large man carrying a small baby on his shoulder.
- The man is carrying the baby across a river.
- To support himself the man is using a wooden stick (staff).

Having brought out these points, go on to give the following information about St Christopher's life to the assembly.

The picture they have been looking at represents one story about St Christopher's life. He was a very tall and strong man. He had been told he could serve God by helping travellers across a dangerous and fast-flowing river.

One night he was carrying a small child across the river when, half-way across, he noticed how heavy the child was and how difficult it was to carry him. The child explained that he was Jesus and that he was so heavy because he was carrying all the worries of the world on his shoulders. Jesus told St Christopher that he would see that this was true by planting his staff into the ground on the other side of the river. By morning it would have started to grow. And it did.

After this experience St Christopher was believed to have gone to the city of Lycia where he preached the words of Jesus until he was put to death by Darius for refusing to deny his faith.

His name, Christopher, means Christ-bearer, and it comes from the story you have just told. Next ask the pupils of whom St Christopher is believed to be the patron saint. Bring out the answer: Travellers. Go on to explain that St Christopher is the patron saint of travellers, especially motorists and sailors. You might like to suggest that this could be because of the story you have just told, that he carried Jesus in the form of a baby across a river.

Show the pupils the medallion. Ask why people wear them. Bring out the answer: They believe it will keep them safe when travelling. Go on to explain that the medallion is thought to keep you safe according to the belief that if you see a picture of St Christopher on a particular day, you will not die that day. As the St Christopher medallion has a picture of St Christopher on it, so it is supposed to keep you safe.

Conclude the assembly by explaining that all saints have a day on which people traditionally celebrate their life, and that St Christopher's feast day is 25 July. In a reorganization of the calendar of saints carried out by the Roman Catholic church in the 1960s, St Christopher was removed from the calendar, but many people still celebrate his feast day. Finally, point out that on 25 July this year the pupils might like to think about the story of St Christopher.

Related assemblies None

Doubting Thomas

Theme   St Thomas

Date   In the last week of the Autumn term

Materials
- A pair of training shoes
- A sheet of paper with the following words of a Christmas song written on it:

  Christmas is coming and the geese are getting fat,
  Please spare a penny for the old man's hat,
  If you haven't got a penny, a ha'penny will do,
  If you haven't got a ha' penny, God bless you.

Before the assembly select a volunteer from your form to read the words of the Christmas song. It would be a good idea to provide time for him/her to practise the reading.

Assembly organization   Start the assembly by asking the pupils what is special about the date, 21 December. Bring out the answer: It is the shortest day of the year. Go on to explain that as well as being the shortest day, 21 December was also traditionally St Thomas's Day.

Next, tell the pupils a few facts about who St Thomas was. Some points to mention might be:

- He was one of Jesus's disciples.
- He is sometimes called 'doubting Thomas' because when he was first told of Jesus's resurrection he did not believe it (John 20: 24–29).
- St Thomas was believed to have spent part of his life in India and to have preached the teachings of Jesus until his death.
- He was the patron saint of old people.

There are many traditions associated with the feast of St Thomas. Here are some you might like to share with the pupils:

Throwing shoes   On St Thomas's Eve people believed that if you threw a pair of shoes over your shoulder and left them where they fell until morning, you could tell if you would be leaving home within the next year, according to the following signs:

- If the shoes pointed towards the door you would leave home in the next year.
- If the shoes pointed away from the door you would not be leaving home in the next year.

If you wish you could ask for some volunteers to come forward and simulate this tradition as part of the assembly. Try to pick volunteers who would not be worried by the superstitious idea of foretelling their future. Allow each volunteer to throw a pair of training shoes over their shoulder towards a door. Depending on the position they land, decide if the pupil will leave the school in the next year. Perhaps you could also introduce the idea of one shoe facing the door and one facing away from the door; in this case you could suggest that the pupil may or may not leave school in the next year.

Locking teachers out

St Thomas's Day was one of the occasions when it was traditional for school children to rush to school early and lock the school doors to stop the teachers from getting in. The teacher would only be let into school if he/she promised the pupils an immediate holiday. Of course as it was nearly Christmas and the term was due to end anyway, this promise could easily be made by the teacher.

Charity

Go on to point out that St Thomas's Day was also a day for people to give to charity.

Some charitable actions to mention could be:

- In Worcestershire it was traditional for children to go round asking for apples.
- As St Thomas was the patron saint of old people, on this day old people were allowed to go around asking for small gifts of money. This was called 'Thomasing'.
- In Warwickshire poor people would go round asking the local farmers for flour to make their Christmas bread. In exchange the farmers were given a sprig of holly.

These charitable actions were also accompanied by singing the Christmas song. (Ask your volunteer to read out the words of the song.)

Conclude the assembly by reminding the pupils that traditionally 21 December was St Thomas's Day and that this was a time for being charitable and thinking of others. As Christmas approaches they should remember this tradition and not just think of themselves.

(If you wish you could mention that in the 1960s St Thomas's Day was moved by the Catholic Church from 21 December to 3 July, both of which are days on which people believe he may have died, but 3 July was thought to have been the date on which St Thomas's bones were moved to their final resting place.)

Related assemblies None

Additional notes This assembly could be used as the basis for introducing a charity event related to thinking of others at this time of year.

Paul's journey

Theme   St Paul

Date   On or near 29 June

Materials
- 2 chairs

Before the assembly you will need to recruit 18 volunteers from your form to play the following people in a mini-play, and allow them time to practise their parts.

St Paul
Governor Felix
Three members of a ship's crew
Four guards
Six people to form a crowd
Governor Festus
Two people to attack Paul

Assembly organization   Start the assembly by explaining to the pupils that there are many stories about the life of the man whom today's assembly is about, but you want them to watch a short play which illustrates one part of his life. At the end of the play you want someone to tell you who the person was (while you do this, your volunteers should get into their places.)

Narrator   Here we see a man preaching to a crowd of people in a town called Jerusalem. His enemies tried to have him killed, but he was arrested.

○   *Crowd seated on the floor; Paul standing talking to them. Two other people come over and start pushing Paul around. Guards march in and escort Paul away.*

Narrator   This man was taken away and brought before Governor Felix, who ordered that he be kept under arrest.

○   *Guards march over with Paul to where Felix is seated. Paul steps forward to stand in front of Felix. After a few seconds Paul steps back between the guards who march him away to where the second chair is. Paul sits on the chair and the guards stand nearby. Felix leaves the governor's chair.*

Narrator   After some days Governor Festus travelled to see the man so he could try to decide what to do with him.

○   *Festus enters and sits in the governor's chair. Guards march over and collect Paul and then march him over to Festus. Paul steps forward to face Festus.*

Narrator   While the man was in the court of justice facing Festus, he informed Festus that he was a Roman and as such had the right to be tried by the Emperor of Rome. To which Festus replied that he could go to Rome and be tried by the Emperor.

o   *Festus stands and points towards the ship's crew. Paul steps back between the guards. Guards march over with Paul to the ship's crew.*

Narrator   After some time the man was taken by ship to Rome. But on the journey the ship was hit by a terrible storm.

o   *Guards hand Paul over to the ship's crew and march away. Ship's crew sit Paul on the floor and then mime setting sail to begin the journey. Paul and crew mime being at sea during a terrible storm.*

Narrator   During the storm some of the crew planned to kill the man and the other prisoner, but he was such a help to them they changed their minds. Eventually the ship ran aground and sank, but the crew and prisoners managed to swim ashore.

At the end of the mini-play ask the assembly who the man was. Bring out the answer: St Paul. Go on to explain that having been shipwrecked on the island of Malta, St Paul spent some time on the island before completing his journey to Rome. St Paul then spent a number of years in the city of Rome writing letters and preaching the words of Jesus (Acts 21:27– 28:31). What eventually happened to St Paul is not certain, but one story says that he was beheaded during the persecution of the Christians under Emperor Nero in AD 62.

Conclude the assembly by telling the pupils that St Paul is the patron saint of tent-makers and saddlers, as he himself was believed to have originally been a tent-maker in Tarsus. He has two feast days, one is 29 June, which he shares with St Peter. He also has a second feast day, on 25 January, which is connected with his conversion on the road to Damascus. If you wish, you could tell the pupils some of the details related to St Paul's conversion (Acts 9: 1–25).

Related assemblies None

Famous people

Throughout history there have been many people whose lives have been a source of inspiration to others. These assemblies provide the opportunity to consider the lives of a few of these inspirational people.

Assembly	Theme
Everest	*All members of a team are of equal importance*
Scott of the Antarctic	*Everyone in a team must do their best*
The lady with the lamp	*Service to others*
Edith Cavell	*Doing what you believe to be right*
The diary of Anne Frank	*Everyone has the right to their beliefs, free from persecution*
Robin Hood	*Protecting the weak*
Twm the highwayman	*Protecting the weak*
Douglas Bader	*Determination in the face of adversity*
King Canute	*Wisdom*

Everest

Theme   All members of a team are of equal importance

Date   On or near 29 May

Materials   ● Large map of the world

Assembly organization   Start the assembly by asking the pupils if they can tell you what famous event took place on 29 May 1953. If no one knows the answer you will need to tell them that at 11.30 on that day Mount Everest was finally conquered and humans reached its summit.

Next explain a little about the mountain itself. Some facts you might like to mention are:

● It is the world's tallest mountain and its height was first measured in 1849 by a team of surveyors mapping India.
● At that time it was known as Peak XV and was measured at 8840 metres high (This was later changed to 8848 metres or 29,028 feet.)
● The leader of the team of surveyors was called General George Everest, after whom the mountain was later named.
● Mount Everest is located on the border between Nepal and Tibet in the Himalayan mountains. (Indicate this area on the large world map.)

Next return to the topic of the 1953 expedition. Ask the assembly who was the first to stand on the summit of Mount Everest. Bring out the answer: Edmund Hillary (later to become Sir Edmund Hillary). He led the final assault on the summit on 29 May. Ask the assembly who was climbing with Hillary on that day. Bring out the answer: Sherpa Tenzing Norgay. (One of the local people who helped all climbing expeditions in the Himalayas.)

Next go on to explain that three days before, on 26 May, two other climbers, Tom Bourdillon and Charles Evans, who were also part of the team, had made an unsuccessful attempt to reach the summit. They undoubtedly provided vital help to Hillary and Tenzing's successful attempt.

Ask the pupils what sort of things these men would have needed to take with them to climb this mountain. Some answers to bring out might be:

● Food
● Ropes (to climb with)
● Tents
● Oxygen (to breathe)

- Warm clothing
- Ladders (to climb across cracks in the ice called crevasses)
- Fuel (to cook with)

Go on to point out that there was in fact tons of equipment that had to be carried to various parts of the mountain to make it possible for Hillary and Tenzing to reach the summit. Explain to the assembly that much of this equipment was carried up the mountain by a team of climbers and local Sherpas.

Now ask the assembly what word describes what was needed for Hillary to reach the summit of Mount Everest. Bring out the answer: Team work. Next ask the pupils what every team must have. Bring out the answer: A leader. Ask the pupils who was the leader of the 1953 Expedition. (If you wish you could ask a member of staff to answer this question.) Bring out the answer: Colonel John Hunt (later to become Lord Hunt).

Point out that Hillary's successful conquest of Mount Everest would not have been possible were it not for the hard work of a large team of mountaineers and Sherpas led by Colonel Hunt.

Conclude the assembly by pointing out that there are many times in school when we have to work together as a team and that these teams will not be successful unless everyone tries their hardest. The efforts of each member of the team are vital to the team's overall success.

Related assemblies Scott of the Antarctic

Scott of the Antarctic

Theme   Everyone in a team must do their best

Date   On or near 1 November

Materials   None

Assembly organization   Start the assembly by asking the pupils if they have heard the saying, or if anyone has ever said to them, 'Pull your weight'. Ask the assembly what they think this saying means. Bring out the answer: To do your best; try your hardest. Go on to explain that in today's assembly you want to talk about a group of people to whom this saying applied literally.

Talk to the assembly about Captain Robert Scott who attempted to lead one of the first teams to the South Pole. Some questions to ask and get answered regarding the South Pole might be:

1 On which continent is it? *Antarctica.*
2 About how far away is it? *Approximately 12,000 miles away.*
3 What is it like there? *Extremely cold, as low as –70°C in winter.*

Explain to the pupils that the final team, which consisted of Scott himself, Dr Wilson, Captain Oates, Lieutenant Bowers and Petty Officer Evans, originally set off for Antarctica in 1910 as part of a much larger group and that it wasn't until 1 November 1911 that Captain Scott finally chose this sledge party (named above) and departed from his base camp on the trip to the South Pole.

He intended that they should pull a sledge with many of the provisions (tents, etc.) most of the way to the Pole and back, a distance of approximately 3000 kilometres. This was obviously going to be a great effort of team work; they would not be able to put up with any member of the team not 'pulling his weight'.

Having struggled for many days, they reached the Pole only to find they had been beaten by a Norwegian. Some questions to ask and get answered about this event might be:

1 Who was the Norwegian who beat them? *Roald Amundson.*
2 What did he use that gave him an advantage? *Dogs.*
3 How do you think Scott and his team felt?

So now they were faced with the long pull home, at the same time knowing that they hadn't reached the Pole first. On the way home the weather was terrible. As they struggled to reach base camp they suffered a number of bad accidents:

- Evans fell into two large crevasses (cracks in the ice) and suffered concussion.
- Wilson suffered from snow blindness and had to be led.
- Oates suffered from frostbite and could barely put one foot in front of the other.

Yet still they struggled on as a team, working together and helping each other, until finally Captain Oates made the ultimate sacrifice to try to help his friends. He realized he could no longer go on and if they stuck with him they would all die. So one morning with the final words 'I am going out now and I may be some time', he walked out and gave his life so that his team (his friends) might succeed.

Conclude the assembly by pointing out that shortly after Oates had given up his life to help his friends, the whole party died. Some of the last words Scott wrote in his diary were:

> *We shall stick it out to the end but we are getting weaker of course and the end cannot be far. It seems a pity but I do not think I can write more ... For God's sake look after our people.*

This is a sad story but it shows how people can work hard as a team to try to achieve something. Finally point out that the pupils may never need to work in a team the way Scott and the others did, but that whenever they have to work in groups or in sports teams, they should always try their hardest for the benefit of the rest of the team. And be sure they 'pull their weight'.

Related assembly Everest

The lady with the lamp

Theme   Service to others

Date   On or near 12 May (Florence Nightingale's birthday)

Materials
- Large map of the world
- Paraffin lamp (if you have one)
- Six pieces of paper, each with one verse of the poem 'The Charge of the Light Brigade' written on it. (The words are given in the Additional notes with this assembly.)

Before the assembly recruit six volunteers from your form and give them time to practise reading a verse of the poem each.

Assembly organization   Start the assembly by explaining to the pupils that you want to talk to them about a person who became famous during the Crimean War, which took place from 1854 to 1856.

Show the assembly where the Crimea is today (part of the Ukraine) and explain that the war started because Britain and France wanted to stop Russia from expanding its empire into what was at that time part of the Turkish (Ottoman) Empire. Explain to the pupils that although the British and French eventually won the war, the campaign itself was poorly organized and thousands of soldiers were needlessly killed or injured in battle.

Go on to illustrate this point by briefly talking to the pupils about the charge of the Light Brigade, in which 673 men were wrongly ordered to charge a battery of Russian cannons, and from which only 195 returned.

Ask your volunteers at this point to read the verses of 'The Charge of the Light Brigade' and explain to the assembly that this poem was written by Alfred Lord Tennyson to commemorate the tragedy.

Next explain to the assembly that hundreds of wounded soldiers from many battles like the charge of the Light Brigade would have died if it had not been for the work of one woman. Ask the pupils if anyone can tell you who she was. Bring out the answer: Florence Nightingale.

Go on to explain that Florence Nightingale was born in the Italian city of Florence on 12 May 1820 and that she felt she was called by God to find a useful purpose for her life, which she found in nursing. Moved by the reports of the sufferings of soldiers in the military hospitals, she wrote a letter to the Secretary for War offering her service and in late October she was sent with 38 other nurses to the military hospital at Scutari. She arrived just in time to treat the injured from the charge of the Light Brigade.

When she arrived, many patients in the hospital were dying (approximately forty-two out of every hundred), not from their wounds but from disease. Because of the changes she introduced and her tireless efforts, this death rate fell to about two per cent (i.e. approximately two out of every hundred).

At night she would walk the hospital wards (covering about six kilometres) checking on and looking after her patients. Because of this she became known as 'the lady with the lamp'. (If you have an oil lamp you can refer to it at this point.)

After the Crimean War, Florence Nightingale continued her work, and with the money raised as a tribute to her work during the war she founded the Nightingale School for Nurses at St Thomas's Hospital in London. This marked the beginning of professional training for nurses.

Florence Nightingale's contributions to the professional training of nurses was invaluable. Before her work, nurses were untrained members of staff.

In 1907 she was awarded the Order of Merit (which no woman had been awarded before) by King George VII.

Florence Nightingale died on 13 August 1910.

Conclude the assembly by pointing out that Florence Nightingale devoted her life to the services of others and through her work thousands of soldiers' lives were saved and nursing became the professional career it is today.

Related assemblies None

Additional notes 'The Charge of The Light Brigade' by Alfred Lord Tennyson

Verse 1
Half a league, half a league,
Half a league onward,
All in the valley of Death.
Rode the six hundred.
'Forward, the Light Brigade!
Charge for the guns!' he said:
Into the valley of Death
Rode the six hundred.

Verse 2
'Forward, the Light Brigade!'
Was there a man dismay'd?
Not tho' the soldiers knew
Someone had blunder'd:
Their's not to make reply,
Their's not to reason why,
Their's but to do and die
Into the valley of Death
Rode the six hundred.

Verse 3
Cannon to right of them,
Cannon to left of them,
Cannon in front of them
Volley'd and thunder'd;
Storm'd at with shot and shell,
Boldly they rode and well,
Into the jaws of Death,
Into the mouth of Hell
Rode the six hundred.

Verse 4
Flash'd all their sabres bare,
Flash'd as they turn'd in air
Sabring the gunners there,
Charging an army, while
All the world wonder'd:
Plunged in the battery-smoke
Right thro' the line they broke;
Cossack and Russian
Reel'd from the sabre-stroke
Shatter'd and sunder'd
Then they rode back, but not,
Not the six hundred.

Verse 5
Cannon to right of them,
Cannon to left of them,
Cannon behind them
Volley'd and thunder'd;
Storm'd at with shot and shell,
While horse and hero fell,
They that had fought so well
Came thro' the jaws of Death,
Back from the mouth of Hell,
All that was left of them,
Left of the six hundred.

Verse 6
When can their glory fade?
O the wild charge they made!
All the world wonder'd.
Honour the charge they
made!
Honour the Light Brigade,
Noble six hundred!

Edith Cavell

Theme   Doing what you believe to be right

Date   On or near 12 October

Materials   • Six sheets of paper, each with one of the following sentences written on it:

1   Edith Cavell was born on 4 December 1865.
2   While she was working in Brussels, Edith's father became ill.
3   Edith Cavell became matron of a hospital in Brussels. She took up her post in September 1907.
4   The German army occupied Brussels.
5   For many months, Edith helped allied soldiers escape the German army.
6   Eventually Edith and a number of her Belgian helpers were captured.

Before the assembly pick six volunteers from your form and give them time to practise reading one of the above sentences each.

Assembly organization   At the start of the assembly, explain to the pupils that you want them to listen to the life story of a very brave and courageous woman. Ask the six volunteers to read out their information. After each of the six readings you might like to add the following additional information.

Additional information

Sentence 1
Edith was born in a small village near Norwich in England. Her father was a local vicar.

Additional information

Sentence 2
Edith returned home to look after her father and because of this she decided to become a nurse.

Additional information

Sentence 3
Some years after taking up her job in Brussels, World War I started, when the heir to the Austro-Hungarian Empire, Archduke Franz Ferdinand, was assassinated on 28 June 1914 in Sarajevo.

Additional information

Sentence 4
In 1914, following a large battle at Mons, the German army occupied the Belgian city of Brussels. Edith Cavell stayed in her hospital and looked after casualties from both armies.

Additional information

Sentence 5

For many months after the fall of Brussels, Edith Cavell helped hundreds of Allied soldiers escape across the Dutch border to avoid capture by the Germans. The Germans became very suspicious of Edith Cavell, but she continued to help Allied soldiers escape. This placed her own life, and the lives of those who helped her, in great danger.

Additional information

Sentence 6

Edith Cavell admitted her activities in court and said she had helped up to 200 soldiers escape (in actual fact she had probably helped nearer to 1000 soldiers). She was found guilty. On 12 October 1915 she was shot by a German firing squad.

In her last few days when she was told she would always be remembered as a heroine, Edith Cavell said 'Don't remember me like that, think of me only as a nurse who tried to do her duty.'

Conclude the assembly by pointing out that Edith Cavell was a very brave and courageous person who did what she felt was right in spite of the danger to herself. She was even prepared to face her own death by firing squad. Because of this she was known as 'one of the angels of Mons'.

Hopefully we will never face the dangers Edith Cavell faced, but we should try to follow her example and always do what we know is right, no matter what the cost.

Related assembly   Into the lions' den

Additional notes   If you wish this assembly could be adapted to cover the theme of Remembrance Sunday, if you concentrated on Edith Cavell's role in treating the casualties of the war and her courage in helping the soldiers escape.

The diary of Anne Frank

Theme Everyone has the right to their beliefs, free from persecution

Date No specific date

Materials None

Assembly organization Start the assembly by asking the pupils who was Anne Frank. Bring out the answer: A girl who wrote a diary and died during World War II. Go on to point out that Anne and her family were forced to hide in the attic of a building in Amsterdam, which is in Holland. They had to hide there all day, every day, for two years, making as little noise as possible. Not only did they have to remain quiet but their food supplies were limited as much of their food was smuggled to them at great risk to the people bringing it. During this time Anne wrote a secret diary of her feelings. After eight months of living like this she wrote:

> *We have eaten so many brown beans and haricot beans that I can't bear the sight of them any more.*

Ask the pupils what happened to Anne. Bring out the answer: She died in a concentration camp in 1945, as did most of her family and the other people who were in hiding with her. Of Anne's family only her father survived.

Next ask the assembly what terrible crime Anne and her family had committed that they had to hide, and when found, were killed? Go on to answer this question by explaining that during World War II, Adolf Hitler organized for six million Jewish people (like Anne and her family) from all over Europe to be put to death merely because they were Jewish.

Then point out that this sort of irrational hatred of people did not only happen during World War II but regrettably happens all the time. Some further examples you might like to mention might be:

South Africa From 1948 the South African government segregated its people under a system called apartheid, banning groups of people from living and working in certain areas. They even banned people from going and sitting on certain beaches. During this time many people were imprisoned and even died for doing little wrong, only opposing this law. The most famous of these people were Nelson Mandela, who was imprisoned for 26 years, and Steve Biko, who died while under arrest. What was it about these people that meant they were treated in this way? They were black.

Northern Ireland During the 1970s, 1980s and 1990s, groups of people in Northern Ireland were shooting others for little, if any, real reason. One group in 1993 even planted a bomb which killed two young boys (Jonathan Ball and Tim Parry) in the English town of Warrington. Although the origins behind these actions are not simple, in the end it seemed that people were being killed merely because they were Roman Catholic or Protestant. Certainly there was no reason for the two boys to die.

Yugoslavia During the mid 1990s, groups of people in Yugoslavia started to fight each other because of ancient differences, and thousands of them died. Some of these people died in battles but many civilians were killed, it would seem, merely because they were from the 'wrong' group; even children were injured and killed.

Once again a young girl (called Zlata Filipovic) wrote a diary of her experiences during the war in Sarajevo. In it she wrote of a friend's death:

> *Nina, an innocent eleven-year-old little girl – the victim of a stupid war. I feel sad. I cry and wonder why? She didn't do anything. A disgusting war has destroyed a young girl's life.*

Again, although the origins and reasons behind these killings were involved and complicated, in the end, men, women and children, it would appear, were killed for no apparent reason or military objective. At this point you might like to mention some of the facts relevant to any recent troubles of this type which have been mentioned in the news.

Conclude the assembly by pointing out that these are all examples of 'humankind's inhumanity to humankind', and for these sorts of things to stop, everyone must realize that people have the right to their own beliefs and way of life, no matter what the colour of their skin, their religion or beliefs. They should be able to live the way they choose free from harassment (provided they are not breaking the law or harming anyone else).

Related assemblies None

Robin Hood

Theme   Protecting the weak

Date   No specific date

Materials   None

Assembly organization   Start the assembly by explaining that you are going to make a series of statements about a famous legendary person from British history, and that after each one you want them to try and guess who they think the person is. I suggest you use the following list of statements:

- He was a murderer.
- He was a poacher.
- He was one of the first highwaymen.
- He was an outlaw.
- He was the greatest archer.
- He lived in Sherwood Forest.

After each statement ask a few pupils if they know who the character is. Once the pupils have guessed the name Robin Hood, go on to explain a little more about some of the statements you have made. A few points to mention might be:

- Robin Hood was a character who some legends say became an outlaw when he shot one of the King's deer.
- He also shot a forester who threatened his life.
- After this he went to live and hide in Sherwood Forest where he robbed the people as they passed along the forest paths.

So why do we remember Robin Hood and think of him as a good person, not the evil and nasty poacher, robber and murderer the legends say he was?

Ask the assembly what it is Robin Hood is most famous for doing. Bring out the answer: He was believed to have robbed the rich and given the money to the poor.

At this stage you might like to ask the pupils to name some of Robin Hood's outlaws and tell them a little more about the stories surrounding each character. Ask the pupils who was the King of England at the time Robin Hood was believed to have lived. Bring out the answer: Richard I (Richard the Lionheart). Ask the pupils who was the King's brother. Bring out the answer. Prince John.

Go on to explain that Robin Hood was believed to have lived in England while King Richard was away fighting the Crusades and that the King's evil brother, John, was left in charge. Prince

John and his knights forced the people to pay high taxes and that is why Robin Hood took money from the rich and paid it back to the poor.

Remind the assembly that Robin Hood is mainly remembered for the good things that he did and not the bad. He defended the weak and protected them from the bullies that were around at that time.

Conclude the asssembly by pointing out that it is far better to be remembered as Robin Hood is, for protecting the weak, than for being a bully like Prince John.

Related assembly   Twm the highwayman

Twm the highwayman

Theme	Protecting the weak
Date	No specific date
Materials	None
Assembly organization	Explain to the assembly that you want to tell them some stories about a legendary highwayman, a Welshman called Twm Sion Cati. You would like them to listen closely to the stories and to try to think of what other famous character he reminds them.
The cauldron	One day Twm met a very poor man who wanted to buy a cauldron (large cooking pot). Twm told him he could take him to get one for free. He took the man into a shop and told the shopkeeper (who was dishonest) that one of his cauldrons had a small hole in it. To help the shopkeeper find the hole, Twm suggested that he could place the cauldron over his head, then he would be able to see the hole. While the shopkeeper searched in vain for the hole with the pot on his head, Twm and the poor man left the shop with a brand new pot.
The saddle-bag	One day Twm was furious with the cruelty and wickedness of a fellow highwayman, so he decided that he would teach him a lesson. Twm disguised himself as a farmer and rode on an old shabby horse into an area where the other highwayman often ambushed people. On the horse, by his side, Twm had a saddle-bag full to the point of bursting.
	The other highwayman sprang out and held Twm at gunpoint. Twm pretended to be terrified, but instead of handing over the saddle-bags when he was told to, he threw them into the bushes. The cruel highwayman climbed into the bushes after Twm's bags, which he hoped would be full of money, only to find them full of shells. While he did this Twm leapt from his old horse and rode off with the highwayman's beautiful mare, it's saddle-bags full of stolen money.
The disappearing horse	On one occasion Twm took a valuable horse to a crooked horse-dealer, who, as usual, offered a price well below the market value. Twm pretended to be somewhat reluctant to go ahead with the sale, but the horse-dealer pressed the money into Twm's hand. Twm pointed out that he was concerned that the horse did have one fault. The dealer, laughing, asked Twm to show him what the fault was. Twm agreed to show the problem to the man, climbed onto the horse and said, 'The problem is that the horse disappears.' At this, he dug his heels into the horse and rode away with the dealer's money.

Ask the assembly what other character the stories about Twm reminded them of. Bring out the answer: Robin Hood. Go on to point out that, like Robin Hood, Twm's victims were supposed to have been people who were thought to be dishonest themselves. Unlike the legends of Robin Hood, however, Twm may have been a real person. His true name was Thomas Jones and he lived from 1530 to 1609. In 1559 Twm was given an official pardon, perhaps because he had been mistaken for other highwaymen.

Conclude the assembly by reminding the pupils that, like Robin Hood, Twm was a character who did not pick on the weak and in fact often stuck up for them and helped them. Both characters are remembered more for the good side of their behaviour than the bad things they were supposed to have done. Finally point out to the pupils that they, like Twm or Robin Hood, should not pick on the weak and should not bully people less fortunate than themselves. It is far better to help and protect those less fortunate than yourself.

Related assembly   Robin Hood

Douglas Bader

Theme   Determination in the face of adversity

Date   In the week of 21 February (Bader's birthday)

Materials • Nine small pieces of paper, each with one of the following bits of information written on it:

1 He was born on 21 February 1910 in a house in St John's Wood, London.
2 In 1928 he joined the RAF where he showed himself to be an outstanding sportsman at cricket, rugby and hockey. He also became a member of an RAF aerobatics display team.
3 In 1931 he was involved in a plane crash which resulted in both his legs being amputated.
4 When fitted with his artificial legs he was told he would never walk again without the help of a stick. Not only did he walk without a stick, he also played tennis, squash, swam and eventually even flew again.
5 In 1939 he was taken back into the RAF and given control of a flight, squadron and eventually five squadrons of fighter planes.
6 The tactics he helped develop undoubtedly contributed to Britain's victory in the Battle of Britain.
7 In 1941, when the RAF went on the offensive over France, he was shot down and captured. For many people that would have been the end of their part in the war, but not for him.
8 He continued to escape from a number of prisoner-of-war camps, eventually ending up in the famous prison camp of Kolditz Castle.
9 Because of his bravery the RAF awarded him the DSO (Distinguished Service Order) and Bar, and the DFC (Distinguished Flying Cross) and Bar. (Teacher note: The Bar means he was awarded the medal twice for two separate actions.)

Before the assembly select nine volunteers from your form to read the above statements and give them time to practise.

Assembly organization   Start the assembly by explaining that today you want them to listen to a number of facts about the life of a famous British pilot. At the end of the nine readings you would like someone to try to tell you the name of the pilot. Ask your volunteers to read out their statements in the correct order (numbers 1 to 9). Ask the assembly if they can tell you who the person is. Bring out the answer: Douglas Bader. At this point you might like to go back and elaborate on some of the nine statements that have been read out.

Ask the pupils if they had to use one word to describe Douglas Bader and the way he lived his life, what would it be. Some examples to bring out might be:

determined　brave　heroic　independent

Go on to explain how some of these terms apply to his life and how the pupils could benefit from the same qualities.

Determination　When he lost his legs it would have been easy for Douglas Bader to give up and not to have made anything of his life, but he was determined to make the best of his life. Very few of us ever face problems anything like those he faced, but with a little more determination, perhaps we could make a greater success of our lives.

Independence　It would have been very easy for Douglas Bader to rely on other people to help him, but he wanted to be independent and help himself. Perhaps we could also benefit from a little more independence and rely less on other people to come and help us.

Go on to quote the statement once made by Joseph Kennedy (father of the American president), 'When the going gets tough, the tough get going'. Explain that when faced with tremendous difficulties, Douglas Bader did not just give up and say 'It's not fair' or 'I cannot do it', etc., etc. He just got going and tackled the problems he faced and made a great success of his life.

Conclude the assembly by pointing out to the pupils that hopefully none of them will ever face the difficulties Douglas Bader suffered, but if we all tackled our own problems with some of the independence and determination he showed, we might be able to overcome many of them and so make a greater success of our own lives.

Related assemblies　None

Additional notes　If you wish, you could also use this assembly as part of a Remembrance Day assembly by concentrating on Bader's bravery.

King Canute

Theme Wisdom

Date No specific date

Materials
- Seventeen large sheets of paper, each with one word from the following saying written on it in large letters:

  The fool doth think he is wise, but the wise man knows himself to be a fool.

- Two sheets of paper, each with one of the two legends of King Canute (below) written on it.

Before the assembly you will need to select two volunteers from your form to read the two alternative legends of King Canute and allow them time to practise.

Assembly organization Start the assembly by asking for 17 volunteers to come to the front. Give each of them one word from the above saying. (Make sure the words are not given out in the correct order.) Then ask for a volunteer to come and rearrange the words to produce a quote from Shakespeare's play *As You Like It*. (For younger pupils a member of staff could be asked to rearrange the words.)

Having rearranged the words to produce the above saying, go on to explain its meaning to the assembly. One possible interpretation would be:

A wise (sensible) person knows what they can and cannot do, while a foolish (silly) person thinks they can do anything.

Next go on to explain to the assembly that you want them to listen to two legends about a famous king. Ask your volunteers to read the two legends, one after the other.

Legend 1 There was once a famous king who lived over one thousand years ago. He wanted to show his people how powerful he was. He told the members of his court that he could stop the waves of the sea from coming up the beach. He went down to the beach and sat in a chair at the water's edge and commanded the waters to stop. He was unable to stop the tide and eventually had to move.

Legend 2 There was once a famous king who lived over one thousand years ago. He wanted to show his people that he was not all powerful and that his powers were limited. He told the members of his court that he could prove that his powers were limited as he was unable to control the movements of the tide. He went down to the beach and sat in a chair at the water's edge and commanded the waters to stop. As he predicted he was unable to stop the tide and eventually had to move.

After the two legends have been read to the assembly ask the pupils which famous king the legends were about. Bring out the answer: King Canute.

Next go on to ask the pupils in which of the legends was King Canute showing himself to be a fool. Bring out the answer: Legend 1.

Go on to explain that by claiming he was able to control the movements of the tides, something he clearly couldn't do, King Canute was making a fool of himself. In Legend 2 he was showing himself to be a wise man pointing out the limits of the things he could do. (If you wish you could point out that Legend 2 is believed to be the one that is correct and that King Canute was supposedly quite a wise king.)

Conclude this part of the assembly by pointing out that having wisdom means you know what you are capable of and do not claim to be able to do things you clearly cannot.

Next explain to the assembly that you want to talk about another famous king who is well known for his wisdom: King Solomon. His wisdom was well known thousands of years ago.

There are a number of stories related to King Solomon's wisdom in the Bible (1 Kings 3 and 1 Kings 4: 29–34). Perhaps a suitable example to use might be when Solomon judges a difficult case (1 Kings 3: 16–28). You could point out the main facts of this story:

- Two women came to see Solomon for him to settle an argument.
- They both lived in the same house.
- Both women claimed that a baby was theirs.
- Solomon instructed his guards to take the baby away and cut it in half.
- At this, one of the women cried and said the baby should be given to the other woman.
- Solomon told his guards to give the baby to the woman who was crying.

Go on to explain that Solomon had solved the problem using his wisdom. He knew that the real mother would not allow the baby to be cut in half.

Conclude the assembly by pointing out to the pupils that having wisdom means not only that you know what things you are capable of doing, but that you can also solve the problems that you face through life. Wisdom comes from what you have learnt – not only the knowledge (facts) you learn at school but also the experiences you have through life and the knowledge they give you.

Related assembly   Fools rush in